EPIC ATHLETES
ALEX MORGAN

EPIC ATHLETES
ALEX MORGAN

Dan Wetzel

Illustrations by Cory Thomas

SQUARE
FISH

Henry Holt and Company

New York

SQUARE FISH

An imprint of Macmillan Publishing Group, LLC
120 Broadway, New York, NY 10271
mackids.com

Our books may be purchased in bulk for promotional, educational,
or business use. Please contact your local bookseller or the Macmillan
Corporate and Premium Sales Department at (800) 221-7945 ext. 5442 or
by email at MacmillanSpecialMarkets@macmillan.com.

Library of Congress Cataloging-in-Publication Data
Names: Wetzel, Dan, author.
Title: Epic athletes: Alex Morgan / Dan Wetzel.
Description: New York : Henry Holt and Company, 2019. |
Audience: Ages: 8–12.
Identifiers: LCCN 2018039049 | ISBN 978-1-250-25071-1 (paperback)
| ISBN 978-1-250-29585-9 (ebook)
Subjects: LCSH: Morgan, Alex (Alexandra Patricia), 1989– —Juvenile
literature. | Women soccer players—United States—Biography—Juvenile
literature. | FIFA Women's World Cup (2011 : Germany) |
Olympic Games : (30th : 2012 : London, England)
Classification: LCC GV942.7.M673 W47 2019 | DDC 796.334092 [B] —dc23
LC record available at https://lccn.loc.gov/2018039049

Originally published in the United States by Henry Holt and Company
First Square Fish edition, 2020
Book designed by Elynn Cohen
Square Fish logo designed by Filomena Tuosto

3 5 7 9 10 8 6 4 2

AR: 6.5 / LEXILE: 950L

For Caitlin

EPIC ATHLETES
ALEX MORGAN

1
A Dream Come True

THEY FOUGHT FOR 123 minutes. They fought through ninety minutes of regulation. They fought through thirty minutes of extra time. And now they were fighting both exhaustion and each other in the third minute of stoppage time, the extra few minutes added to the clock to account for injury or substitution delays.

To call it a fight wasn't an exaggeration. The women's national soccer teams of the United States and Canada had clawed and grabbed and kicked and battled. They knocked each other down in the open field. They banged into each other contesting balls in the air. They were ferocious and physical, moving back and forth and back again. Anyone who says soccer is a noncontact sport has never really played, and certainly not at this level, in the semifinals of the 2012 London Olympics.

The Canadians led three times during the match. The Americans caught up three times. It was that kind of game, 1–0 then 1–1, 2–1 then 2–2, 3–2 and now 3–3 with just thirty seconds remaining of stoppage time. If no one scored in the next half-minute, the game would go to penalty kicks, with the winner advancing to the gold medal game against Japan.

For Alex Morgan, this was more than just another game. Growing up in Diamond Bar, California, she dreamed of becoming an Olympian even before she knew what sport she wanted to play. She settled early on soccer, of course, even penning a note to her mother when she was eight about how she was going to be a professional player. Everyone thought it was cute. Alex wasn't kidding.

She climbed her way up the ranks of youth soccer. She played on her local recreational team until she was fourteen and didn't join a travel club until she reached high school. At sixteen she made the US under-17 women's national team. At eighteen she enrolled at the University of California, Berkeley on a full scholarship. Now it was 2012, and she was twenty-three years old and not just a starter, but a star on the US Women's National Team (USWNT).

Her dream was coming true. Except, in that moment, it didn't feel like it.

Just a year prior, Alex played for the United States in the 2011 FIFA Women's World Cup. In the final against Japan, she scored the game's first goal and assisted on another. However, Japan came back to tie the score and eventually force a penalty kick shootout. The Japanese won 3–1 on penalty kicks to win the World Cup. Alex and her teammates were crushed. It was the toughest loss of their lives. It was a reminder of how small the difference is between glory and defeat.

Now, one year later, Alex could feel the same thing happening in the Olympics—that the game was headed to a shootout. Victory was slipping from her grasp, and she was here to win. So were her teammates. They believed the United States had the best soccer team in the world. They needed to prove it, though. That meant beating Canada.

Alex was tall, fast, and talented. She would

record twenty-eight goals and twenty-one assists in 2012, leading the USWNT in both categories. She was young, but she expected herself to deliver in the big moments of games. This was the biggest of moments. No one on the team was interested in letting an Olympic final berth be decided on penalty kicks, where anything could happen. They'd been through that heartbreak in the World Cup. They couldn't have it happen again. Alex knew what she had to do.

"I'm a forward," Alex said. "And as a forward, we are supposed to score."

If the World Cup is the ultimate stage in soccer, the Olympics are only slightly less significant. Every kid around the world grows up dreaming of winning an Olympic gold. Now, a long way from those rec fields in California, here was Alex's chance. The game took place in Manchester, England, at a stadium called Old Trafford, which is home to the famed Manchester United Football Club. Since the stadium has hosted so many great games and great players over the years, it's been dubbed the "Theatre of Dreams."

The US rivalry with Canada also added to the pressure of the moment. Along with Japan, Canada was the United States' chief competition at the time. They played each other often, both during exhibition games, called "friendlies," and during the World Cup qualifying matches. Many elite Canadian players also compete on club, or travel, teams in the United States as they grow up, seeking top competition. On her own club team, Alex was even teammates with Christine Sinclair, Canada's captain and best player. Sinclair had scored all three of Canada's goals in the Olympic game and was doing everything she could to will Canada to victory.

Familiarity and friendships meant nothing during this game. The stakes were too high. No one was backing down.

"I just wanted to beat Canada so bad," Alex said.

After all those minutes of playing on the field, Alex was exhausted, but undeterred. She was banged up, but she wouldn't let it bother her. The US had to win. So with thirty seconds remaining, when teammate Heather O'Reilly got the ball on the right flank and lobbed a cross into the goal box, Alex Morgan was focused: "I knew it was our last chance."

She tracked the ball as it soared across the field. She thought about what she needed to do. "Get in front of your player," Alex told herself. "Get your head or some body part on the ball."

Six yards in front of the center of the net, she did just that, out-leaping two defenders—one in front of her, one coming in from behind. Just as she had trained and practiced for years and years, she timed the jump perfectly. As she reached the top of her leap, the ball struck her forehead. She flicked it toward the goal.

The Canadian goalie made a critical error. She either could have stayed back and defended the goal line, or come forward and tried to punch the ball away before Alex got her head on it. Instead the goalie hesitated for a split second, uncertain of what to do. As a result, she took two steps forward, then tried to retreat to the line. The mistake gave Alex the chance to make her move.

Alex's header sailed just over the outstretched arms of the leaping Canadian goalie and just under the crossbar. It was the perfect shot. Anything just slightly higher or slightly lower would have been saved. This one wasn't.

Goooooaaaaaallllll!

"Oh, it's in!" the announcer screamed. "Alex Morgan has done it! Barely thirty seconds to go!"

United States 4, Canada 3.

Alex was knocked to the ground on the play, and when she got back to her feet she was too tired to run off to the sideline even to celebrate with her teammates. Old Trafford erupted into cheers, and the Canadians fell to their knees in disappointment and exhaustion. As the other American players raced toward Alex in excitement, she simply stood there with her arms raised and a smile on her face. Her teammates embraced her. They hugged. They laughed. They told one another "I love you." Soon Alex found herself actually crying, something she wasn't used to doing on a soccer field.

That's how tired she was. Moments later the game was over. The United States was headed to the Olympic finals to play Japan.

"I can't recall ever feeling this way after scoring a goal," said Alex that night. Scoring it, she said, was the product of years of hard work. Not just training and perfecting her header, but all the wind sprints, all the weight lifting, all the work. "It was about who is the fittest, who is the strongest," Alex said.

Days later, the US would defeat Japan 2–1 in the Olympic finals at Wembley Stadium in London, exacting a measure of revenge for their World Cup defeat the year before. Alex had an assist. When it was over, she climbed a podium, had a gold medal draped around her neck, and proudly listened as "The Star Spangled Banner" rang out into the London night.

Alex Morgan's soccer dream was now very much real.

2
Early Years

ALEXANDRA PATRICIA MORGAN was born on July 2, 1989, in a hospital in San Dimas, California, about thirty miles east of Los Angeles. She was the third child and third daughter to Pamela and Michael Morgan. Her oldest sister, Jenny, was six, and Jeri was four. With two daughters already, her parents had been hoping for a son. Since her dad had picked out the name Alexander for a boy, they decided to name their third daughter Alexandra.

Michael owned a construction company and the

family lived in Diamond Bar, California, which was a pleasant suburb of fifty thousand residents. When people think of Southern California, they often think about the beach, but Diamond Bar is at least an hour's drive from the Pacific Ocean. It is dominated by hills, canyons, and tightly packed neighborhoods. It is more of your classic Los Angeles suburb, with nice houses, quiet streets, and lots of shopping centers. The Morgans had a swimming pool and were always inviting friends over. Or they'd walk through Sycamore Canyon Park and pick tadpoles out of the creek. For Alex and her sisters, it was an ideal place to grow up—safe and fun—where you could ride bikes through the winding streets and know almost all the other kids. Then there were the sports.

"Growing up on the West Coast, I think there was so much opportunity to play," Alex said. "Most sports were available to us. I know that isn't always the case, especially for girls, everywhere in America and certainly not around the world. We were lucky."

The Morgan family was a constant presence in the Diamond Bar recreational sports leagues. They'd play almost any sport: softball, volleyball, track, basketball, and of course, soccer. It seemed like the entire family was in a constant state of motion, racing from one practice to the next, one game to another. And that was just the organized leagues. The girls and the other kids from the neighborhood would also get pick-up games going. When Alex's dad got home from work, he'd play catch with the girls out in the yard, or take everyone to local Anaheim Angels baseball games. For a few years, the family had season tickets. On other nights, the family would compete in ferocious board games, with ultracompetitive Alex wanting to win every time.

As the youngest, Alex was often in her older sisters' shadows. She loved them both, but all sisters argue and fight with each other sometimes. Constantly being referred to as "Jeri's kid sister" or "Jenny's baby sister" made Alex want to stand out. That didn't take long in sports. Both Jenny and Jeri were good athletes. Alex was on another level, though— better than people were used to seeing in Diamond Bar. First off, she was fast. By the time she was five or six, she could beat most of the kids in her neighborhood in a foot race, and that included the boys. There was nothing Alex liked more than beating boys, especially ones a year or two older. She wasn't just fast for a girl. She was fast. Period.

Alex was also an excellent softball player, which was her first love. She played on teams coached by her dad. She had excellent hand-eye coordination, and when she hit the ball she would dash around the bases with ease. Soccer eventually became her favorite sport; she found the constant movement and opportunity to showcase her speed exhilarating.

Alex played in the Diamond Bar rec leagues, under the direction of the American Youth Soccer Organization (AYSO). She was so fast at such a young age she was nicknamed "Mighty Mouse." Many girls by the time they are eight or nine have begun playing travel, or club, soccer. The teams are well organized. There is a full-time coach. You need to try out to make the team. The uniforms are often cool. Sometimes they are affiliated with big-name soccer teams, whether Major League Soccer (MLS) teams in the United States, such as the Columbus Crew or the LA Galaxy, or from Europe, such as Liverpool Football Club or Bayern Munich. Practices can be two or three times a week, with games on the weekend. Sometimes there are out-of-town tournaments where everyone stays in a hotel and you might play two or three times in a weekend. At the highest levels, you compete regionally across states or even nationally. It's fun. It can also be a serious, and stressful, business.

Alex didn't play club soccer. She played rec and continued on as a multisport athlete—track, basketball, and still some softball. "I didn't want to commit to one sport," Alex said. "I had fun playing all of them." She wasn't getting the best training or facing the toughest competition in soccer, but that didn't mean she wasn't taking her development seriously. Her father took coaching lessons to learn the sport. They bought a small goal for their yard and he would put Alex through lots of drills, especially focusing on shooting the ball to precise targets. She also continued to run, both on a track team and doing speed drills with a private coach. Mostly though, she got to play soccer with her friends and develop a true love of the game. Occasionally, her father had to push her to keep working, but Alex would almost always respond positively.

During her years in middle school, Alex dominated her rec league. She was practicing every day and had so much physical ability, speed, and skill that the other kids couldn't keep up. She could score almost any time she wanted. Rec sports are intended mostly for fun and by this point it was clear: Alex needed to go bigger if she was going to maximize her potential.

"I knew if I was going to get better, I had to challenge myself," she said.

The difference between rec soccer and club

soccer is considerable, though. Alex was thirteen when she first tried out for a nearby club team. She was used to playing with her friends, being the star, and winning games. But all those goals she scored in rec soccer no longer mattered. She didn't make the cut. The coaches believed she had potential, but she was extremely raw. Soccer requires intricate skills to deftly handle the ball, whether it is a first touch when receiving a pass or a step-over to win a one-on-one matchup. These are abilities soccer players hone over years of repetition. There is no shortcut, even when you are Alex Morgan. She couldn't just run by everyone. The other girls had been playing club soccer for four, five, even six years or more. Alex was given a spot on the team as a practice player and essentially told that if she worked out for a full year with the club, she might be able to get into games at some point.

"Reality slapped me in the face," Alex said.

Practicing but not playing didn't sound like much fun, but Alex took what she was offered. She vowed to come to training every day, get better, and prove herself to the coaches. It was tough. Practice was a thirty-minute drive from her home. The other kids knew the drills better. She didn't have any friends on the team. She was the new girl and didn't find anyone who was particularly friendly to her. Being a thirteen-year-old is never easy, and practicing without any support from others on the team made the situation even more difficult.

For three months, she trained. While she thought she was improving, the coaches didn't think she had improved enough to play in any actual games. She never got a chance to prove herself on the field. None of the other girls tried to be her friend. She was lonely and frustrated. Soccer had always been a source of joy for her. This was the opposite. It wasn't going to work.

As Alex turned fourteen and entered high school, she knew she had to find a club team where she fit in. Despite setbacks, she refused to give up on her dream. That's when she heard about Cypress Elite Futbol Club in Orange County, California. It had a good reputation. She went to an open tryout and walked on the field a bit uncertain and very anxious. She needed to make this work. She had no idea what would happen. Was she going to be cut again? Was she going to be told she wasn't good enough? Standing there watching was coach Dave Sabet, who was quickly amazed at this raw but extremely fast and physically skilled prospect.

"She just blew by all my club players," Coach

Sabet told *USA Today*, describing Alex's first tryout. "But the thing about her was, she didn't have any sort of idea. No skill. She just had phenomenal speed."

Coach Sabet didn't hesitate, though. Speed was enough. With her natural talent, she was clay that he could mold. Alex made the team. The challenge wasn't over. She was playing with and against kids who had spent about half their lives playing elite club soccer. They weren't just honing their technical skills, but at this point they were learning how to play tactically. A great soccer player is someone who knows how to move without the ball, where to place the ball when passing, and how to not just connect with their teammates but how to play off them. You have to learn to think about the game and understand in advance how a play will unfold so you are in position when the ball comes to you.

Alex also had to adapt to the way the structure of soccer games change as players get older. Little kids will start by playing games of four players versus four players with no goalie. The ability to make a simple cut can make someone a star, especially when some opponents aren't paying attention— instead picking a daisy or doing a cartwheel, as younger kids are prone to distraction. As they get older, children switch to seven versus seven or nine versus nine matchups, which require more passing and positioning, but the field isn't as big as professional fields are, and one-on-one moves still can be incredibly important in generating scoring opportunities.

By the time the game moves to the big field and it's eleven versus eleven, it's more about setting up attacks, runs and crosses, or executing set pieces—plays designed by the coach for free or corner kicks. With fewer players in a seven versus seven game, the field is wide open and offense is easier, so scores are typically much higher. In an eleven versus eleven match, the final score is often 1–0. No one can win a game by themselves. If you beat one defender, that's great, but unless it creates space for a shot, it won't mean much. You'll have to quickly beat another defender who has rotated over. This can hurt some players and benefit others.

Alex was a fast study. She immediately connected with her teammates at Cypress Elite. They became fast and lifelong friends. And Dave Sabet became more than a coach. He was a mentor. He was willing to help Alex put in extra work before and after practice. Alex would take any chance she had to dribble through cones, perfect her first touch, or get extra shots on net. She had, Coach Sabet said, speed that you can't teach. She also had an uncanny nose for scoring goals. She was constantly attacking, which isn't something that comes naturally to all players. Sabet believed if she could learn the rest of the game, the sky was the limit.

It took just six months of hard work with Cypress Elite for Alex to burst onto the scene. She was a star, scoring goals and developing seemingly by the week. You couldn't miss her on the field. That spring, Alex was invited to the prestigious Cal South Olympic Development Program. The ODP has camps across the country and is set up to identify the most promising young talent in America. The program features the best of the best.

The ODP invitation was an incredible honor for Alex and a turning point in her life. She was no longer a rec soccer player dreaming of being a national team player such as Mia Hamm or Kristine Lilly. Alex was now on the path to actually joining them. Just getting invited to the ODP camp doesn't mean a player will make the national team. Far from it. There are dozens and dozens of kids at each ODP. Playing there is a good step, though.

By age fifteen, Alex was either practicing or playing soccer almost every day of the week. Each weekend she was off playing games or tournaments around California and sometimes even traveled to other states to compete. She was no longer living the traditional teenage lifestyle. She still went to high school, got good grades, and tried to remain close to her lifelong friends in Diamond Bar, but she was also making social sacrifices. When everyone else at school was hanging out together on Saturday night, she was off playing soccer, usually by herself. Soccer had become her life. It required absolute dedication, but she loved it.

Alex also joined the Diamond Bar High School soccer team, which had a good program and allowed her to play alongside many of her lifelong friends. While most players, even very good ones, have to work their way up through the freshman team or the junior varsity team for a few years, Alex was instantly a starter on the varsity as a freshman, even though she was still developing her tactical skills.

"She had speed, and that enabled her to compete even without some fine touches that some of the older girls possessed," said Kemp Wells, who coached Alex at Diamond Bar High School. "She could also shoot very well. That is something she could always do. She definitely belonged on the field as a starter.

"She wanted to be better, too," Coach Wells said. "She had a drive to improve that was superior to the average player. She had a mentality: 'Nobody is going to outwork me.' You saw it every day in practice. In every drill, she led. She improved rapidly. There was a humility about it. She wasn't satisfied. Sometimes you have a good player that thinks they are great and they stop working. Alex wanted to be great."

Her development continued to be swift. She was All-Conference as a sophomore at Diamond Bar and helped Cypress Elite thrive. The progression of her career was like when someone stands up a row of dominoes and knocks one over, which knocks another over, which knocks another. Cypress Elite and Diamond Bar High led to the ODP, and now the ODP was about to lead to something even bigger . . . college.

3

College Recruitment

ALEX'S PARENTS WERE very supportive. They could also be very strict. While her dad did all he could to foster her athletic ability, he also knew the chance of making a serious living playing professionally—especially for a woman, given the limited number of female pro soccer leagues— was remote. School had to remain a focus. Meanwhile, her mom was a stickler for academics. She had gone back to graduate school to get a master's degree when all three of her girls were under the age of ten. She took classes at night and often studied when the rest of the house was asleep. She wanted her daughters to have that academic base also. Jenny and Jeri were both excellent students. Alex would have to be also. Yes, she was a gifted athlete, but she couldn't play soccer forever. Even a long and successful career has to end at some point. Then what?

Alex agreed, and attacked her academics like she did opposing defenses. She may have spent her high school years racing around California, the United States, and the world, but she kept up with school. She'd study on long drives and plane flights. She'd have her nose in a book before practice and after. She did whatever it took. By her sophomore year in high school, she knew she wouldn't just have an opportunity to go to college, she would likely be going for free on a full athletic scholarship. Nearly every school in America wanted Alex Morgan to play soccer for them. About the only thing that could limit her were her grades. As long as they were good, she was in a great position.

"She was a very strong student," said Coach Wells, who is an English teacher at Diamond Bar High School as well as a soccer coach. "Diamond

Bar is a very rigorous school academically, but she was just a hard worker in all facets of her life. She was soft-spoken off the field, which is different than most people think based on how intense she plays on the field. She was goal driven and that included academics."

Recruiting quickly ramped up for Alex. Letters, campus brochures, and phone calls came in from universities everywhere—North Carolina, Michigan, Texas, and so on. If Alex had been interested in a school and not heard from them, she probably could have just sent the head coach an email and they would have responded immediately. That's what a spot in the Cal South ODP can do for you.

For the Morgans, this was incredible. At fourteen, Alex had wondered if she could even make it at Cypress Elite. Fast forward two years, and now at the age of sixteen she had her pick among the top college soccer programs in the country. If anything, Alex's recruitment was a bit late for a top-line player. Typically, the top college teams will start looking at players as young as thirteen. For Alex, the first challenge was narrowing down the list of schools she would consider. No one has the time to properly analyze, let alone visit, say, fifty schools all over

America. Besides, once you start talking to recruiters, they'll make every place sound perfect, and with good reason—most colleges are incredible places to live and study.

Alex decided she had two main priorities. She wanted to attend a school with great academics, and she wanted to stay in California so she wouldn't be too far from home. That chopped the list considerably, whittling her options down to six schools— University of Southern California, Pepperdine University, University of San Diego, Santa Clara University, Stanford University, and University of California, Berkeley.

Each of the schools offered something special. There were big schools and small schools, private schools and public schools, even schools with religious affiliations. There were schools in Southern California and schools in Northern California. For Alex, the decision was made once she was able to tour Cal Berkeley, which sits just north of Oakland and just east of San Francisco. She was already impressed with the school's academics. She really liked the coaching staff, particularly Head Coach Kevin Boyd, who had built a very strong program that annually reached the NCAA Tournament. Coach Boyd had connected well with Alex through the recruiting process, and she trusted how he would use her in games. She was also comfortable with the other players on the team.

Cal was away from home, but not too far—a six-hour drive. The university is a very liberal place, and the town is vibrant and colorful. Alex loved the free spirits and atmosphere on campus. She thought the students' interest in social activism was inspiring, and liked how they interacted with professors. Mainly, she thought it would be best to have a change of environment. She loved Diamond Bar, but it was a traditional suburb. Berkeley was anything but that. San Francisco and all the culture and diversity it offered were a quick train ride across the Bay. Cal would challenge her and push her forward, both inside and outside of the classroom. One thing she had settled on was trying to find a school that she would want to attend, even if for some reason the sport of soccer no longer existed. Cal was it. She signed a letter of intent as a high school junior and was accepted academically as a senior.

"One of the main reasons I went to Cal is it is one of the top universities in the world," Alex said. "That was an amazing opportunity for me. I feel that is a main reason they have a great athletic program. A lot of kids want a great academic program as well as athletic. I think that attracts people. I think the city of Berkeley is a beautiful city and a fun city to live in for four years."

With her future set, Alex kept thriving on the field. At Diamond Bar High School, she became a star player, which helped her develop different skills. First was leadership. She didn't carry herself as a star. She wanted to be seen as just another player and the team's hardest worker.

"Alex was in ODP and working with the U-17 national team, but she didn't make a big deal about it around the [Diamond Bar] team," Coach Wells said. "She just went and worked hard. As a coach, it's so valuable when your best player is your hardest worker because it makes the other players work hard also. It can be great motivation for everyone and help make everyone better."

As the primary offensive threat on the field, Alex also learned to deal with the other team focusing their defense on her. Everyone knew who Alex was, and opposing teams didn't want her to beat them.

"She was getting double- and triple-teamed," Coach Wells said. "They'd have two players mark her and then shade over another player. Alex became an excellent passer out of necessity. We had a girl on the team who scored a ton of goals because Alex would draw the whole defense over and then she'd pass it across. The girl would sit about eighteen yards out and put balls away. Alex just wanted to win. She didn't care who scored the goals; that was secondary. She would do whatever it took to win."

Diamond Bar's archrival is Walnut High School, which sits in the next town over, just four miles away. Many of the kids know each other from various activities or even from attending elementary schools together. When the schools compete, it's about more than just getting the win. Pride is on the line. When sports schedules are released, all the students mark their calendars, eagerly awaiting the game against their rival.

In one matchup between the two schools, Alex truly showed what a team player she was. In the first half she scored twice and had an assist to give Diamond Bar a 3–0 lead. But there was still a whole half left to play, and Walnut had one great goal scorer that concerned Coach Wells. Diamond Bar would win as long as she didn't have a big second half. At halftime, as Coach Wells spoke to the team about making sure the Walnut player was covered, Alex volunteered to switch to defense if he thought it would help, even though she never played defense. All she wanted to do was win.

"Alex man-marked her the entire second half," Coach Wells said. "She shut her down and we won. She didn't care about scoring; she took on the toughest job and did it."

Alex's senior year was going perfectly. Her Diamond Bar team was winning. Her college choice was set. And she achieved another step toward her dream when her play in the ODP caught the eye of the coaches of the US U-17 women's national soccer team. Her ultimate goal was to play for the senior women's national team, and while U-17 offered no guarantees, it was on the path to getting there. The team featured many of the best players from Alex's age group from across the country. Getting to compete with and learn from the other players gave Alex incredible confidence. In a friendly against a club team from San Diego, she scored a goal and recorded two assists. Alex still had to develop her skills—in soccer the learning process never ends—but she felt she belonged. Everything was falling into place and it seemed nothing could go wrong. But then came a major setback.

One day, Alex was practicing with her U-17 national team in Southern California. They were scrimmaging against a boys' team when Alex tried to chase down an opposing player. As he made a move on her, she tried to adjust. When she planted her right leg, it gave out and she collapsed, feeling a burning pain in her knee. She knew she couldn't walk.

She'd torn her ACL.

Lying crumpled on the ground, she fought back tears, wondering if she would ever play soccer again. Was this it? Was her career finished just as it was beginning? Was all the hard work going to be for naught? Was her dream over?

ACL stands for anterior cruciate ligament. These are the ligaments that basically hold a person's knee together and allow it to bend. It's a serious injury. It is also a common one that doctors know how to fix. A torn ACL requires surgery and then a six-month to one-year rehabilitation process. It requires lots of physical therapy and strengthening drills—but no playing soccer. Recovery can be hard and mundane.

Alex was devastated and scared. Soccer was her life and now she couldn't play it. She also worried about what kind of player she would be after rehab.

Cal was going to honor her scholarship for now, but would she be as good as before when she returned to the field? The U-17 national team would replace her quickly, at least for the time being. There is always another talented player looking for an opportunity. Then there was Cypress Elite, which had first given her a chance. She was a team captain by then and had been preparing for what would've been her final season playing for the club. Now it was gone. The same was true of Diamond Bar High School and all her old friends. She had wanted to help push the team as far as it could go in pursuit of a state title. Now her senior year season ended after just six games.

Losing the chance to formally compete was hard, but completely missing out on any opportunity to play soccer, even just for fun, was the real blow. She loved soccer and had since she was a little girl. Could she stand to have it out of her life for an extended period of time? Could a person who never stopped moving suddenly deal with not having a packed schedule, instead watching lots of television and reading books?

The surgery went well. Alex poured herself into rehab. For five months she didn't play soccer, although she attended every Cypress Elite practice. She just watched, but she felt being there was important. She was a captain, after all. And these were her friends that she had played alongside for the past few years. They'd sweated together, worked together, traveled together, and, of course, won together.

In restrengthening her knee, Alex said she really strengthened herself mentally and emotionally. Having something she loved taken away and losing out on a bunch of opportunities she had worked toward made her even more focused.

"I think in the long run it was the best thing to happen to my career, which is a strange thing to say," Alex said. "It took not playing for me to realize the passion I had for soccer. I wanted to play in college and professionally. I wanted to play for the national team. Losing soccer for that stretch changed my focus. This wasn't just fun. For me to play as long as I could and at the highest level I could, I needed to really work. I didn't take anything for granted after that."

Every game—and even every practice—was an opportunity now. Soccer, she knew, could end at any moment, and that wasn't a life she wanted to experience ever again.

4

Cal

BEFORE ALEX ARRIVED at Cal Berkeley, she was hit with a shock. Head Coach Kevin Boyd, who had recruited her, resigned from the job. The announcement came out of nowhere, on a calm March day in 2007 during Alex's senior year of high school. Coach Boyd and his wife were about to become parents. Buying a house and raising a child in the Bay Area is very expensive. They felt they needed to move elsewhere. A few weeks later, he was hired as the new women's soccer head coach at Arizona State

University, which is near Phoenix and is a more affordable location for a young, growing family.

Alex understood. Family comes first. Still, she had chosen Cal in part to play for Kevin Boyd. They had developed a good relationship during the recruiting process. She liked Cal's style of play. She believed he would get the most out of her game. Would the new coach like her? Would he or she be patient as Alex returned from her ACL injury? The uncertainly reaffirmed she had made the right choice in picking a school that was about more than just soccer. Cal, she kept reminding herself, was still Cal.

Neil McGuire was hired as the new women's soccer head coach. He grew up in Scotland but had been coaching college soccer in the United States for years, most recently as the head coach of Texas Tech University. He gathered the team and told them he wanted to play aggressively on offense. "We will be a team that attacks," he said. Then he stated his goal for the program: "Win the national championship." Alex was relieved. This was exactly what she wanted to hear.

Injuries tend to create doubt in all athletes. They worry about getting reinjured if they rush back.

Many athletes return, but never reach the same level of play as before the injury occurred. They also need to regain their conditioning, and for a soccer player, their technical skill. There isn't much a player can do without ball skills. The only way to maintain those at the elite level is to work on them almost every single day. Alex didn't want to just play for Cal; she wanted to be a starter and lead the team in goals scored.

As camp began, it was clear her knee was fine. All the rehab and physical therapy had paid off. She wasn't 100 percent and still needed to regain her top speed, but she was fast enough.

"It was easy to see her pure athleticism, but what impressed me the most was her balance and poise in and around the goal, as well as her fierce competitiveness," Coach McGuire said. "I was immediately excited to have the opportunity to work with her."

Then in a practice drill, she stepped wrong and felt her ankle give out as pain shot up her leg. *Not again*, she thought. Just as she was back from the torn ACL, just as her college career was set to start, just as she was playing the game she loved, this happened? Was she destined for months on the sideline, days filled with mundane rehab and physical therapy, all as NCAA soccer went on without her?

Then came relief. Team doctors diagnosed it as just a sprain. The season would begin with her sitting on the bench, watching and receiving treatment, but she might only be out a month. Alex tried to remain positive. She used the time on the bench watching how Coach McGuire wanted the game played.

When she returned in mid-September, she charged into the game as a substitute in the fifty-fourth minute, ready to prove she was for real. Cal lost that day, but Coach McGuire was impressed enough that two days later, Alex started against San Diego State University. Coach McGuire stressed that the starting lineup wasn't set and he would rotate it at some positions. In the fifty-third minute, Alex took a pass from teammate McKenna-Louise McKetty and blasted it in for her first NCAA goal. Cal went on to win 2–0.

Just like that, she was a full-time starter.

Three games later Alex had a hat trick, which means she scored three goals in a single game. The term began in the 1800s at a cricket match in England and now is used throughout sports. In hockey, fans will throw their actual hats onto the ice to honor the player. That doesn't happen much in soccer, but Alex didn't care. It was still September of her freshman season and she was on fire.

"Alex has had a fairly difficult last six months with an ACL tear and an ankle injury," Coach McGuire said. "This is a testament to her work ethic. She did individual practice on goal scoring this week and the work paid off. She's deserving of those goals for sure."

Two days later, Cal traveled to play Santa Clara, which was ranked number one in the country at the time. Santa Clara is also in the Bay Area and thus a big rival of Cal. This was a game Alex had been waiting for, and in the twenty-ninth minute of a scoreless match, she broke free behind the defense and knocked in a goal. It proved to be the game winner as Cal pulled the big upset, winning 2–0.

"Alex has produced a spark we needed," Coach McGuire said.

In late October, Cal traveled to Arizona State, where they played against Coach Boyd and the Sun Devils. The game was emotional for a lot of the Bears, and they played like it, winning 3–1 against their former coach. For Alex, she showed Coach Boyd he was right to recruit her. She scored twice. It was a sign of things to come.

The Bears got on a run beginning in late October and started playing their best soccer. They won six consecutive games to end the season, and while

Alex didn't always score, she learned how to become a better passer and affect games even if she didn't find the net.

Cal entered the NCAA Tournament—a sixty-four-team competition to decide the Division I college soccer champion—ranked eleventh nationally, and defeated Santa Clara in the first round. That set up a game against archrival Stanford, which was ranked second in the country.

The Cal–Stanford rivalry is one of the most intense in college athletics. They both are located in the Bay Area, just on different sides of the Bay. They both have great athletic departments, particularly for women's sports. They are both excellent academic institutions. So like Alex, many of the players are recruited by both schools. It feels as though everyone knows each other. Stanford featured two of Alex's future teammates on the US Women's National Team, Christen Press and Kelley O'Hara. This was big-time college soccer.

The game was intense, with every ball contested. Getting free space was nearly impossible. Both teams wanted to advance in the NCAA Tournament while also ending the season of their rival. Stanford took a 1–0 lead in the thirty-fifth minute and looked like they were going to win as they carried the lead late into the game. Then in the eighty-ninth minute, just before the game was over, Cal won a free kick near midfield.

"We pushed everyone up because we had two minutes left," Alex said. "We were all kind of [going for it]."

Alex tracked and timed the ball perfectly as it soared into the box, rising up in a crowd of players and heading it in to tie the game. Her teammates mobbed her. It was the start of Alex's long tradition of scoring late, meaningful goals. After two hard-fought ten-minute overtime periods, the game went to penalty kicks (or PKs). No one likes seeing a game that has been played so well and for so long decided by penalty kicks. They are a part of soccer, but not the heart of soccer, where every goal is the product of team play.

In a penalty kick shootout, each team alternates taking five shots on the opposing goalie from the penalty spot, which is twelve yards in front of the center of the net. If the game is still tied after five shots, then PKs continue, with each team getting a turn. At that point, it's sudden death: If one team scores and the other doesn't, the game is over. Each player can only take one shot. It is dramatic, and it is high pressure. For the players involved, a single mistake can cost an entire game's worth of hard work. Or in this case, an entire season. And for the teammates watching, it can be even more nerve-racking because you are helpless.

"It's not the best way to determine a winner," Alex said. It's necessary, though, because otherwise games could go on forever, which can be dangerous for exhausted players.

Alex was just a freshman but she immediately volunteered to take one of Cal's penalty kicks. She was the team's leading scorer and she was confident in her ability to make it. Mostly, she didn't want the season to end without her being involved.

"Neil wanted to know who wanted to take PKs, and I'm always fine with PKs," she said. "I'm always up for a PK."

It takes a special mind-set to shoot penalty kicks. Scoring feels more like a relief than an accomplishment. Failing can be crushing. Alex wanted to be one of the players deciding the game, though. She wasn't rattled by the pressure. Shooters have to step up to the penalty spot with a plan. Success is generally about placing the ball where you want it— almost a pass into the net—rather than shooting as hard as possible and losing accuracy.

"Just put the ball in the back of the net," Alex said when describing her strategy. "I don't really look at the goalkeeper. It is more about myself than it is about her. For the most part, I know when I step up where I am going to aim. Obviously if the goalkeeper has a tendency to go early [as in jump to one side or the other in an attempt to guess where the shot is headed], then I know that as well. But for the most part, I have a clear idea where I am going to go."

In the first of five rounds, Stanford scored and Cal didn't, giving Stanford a 1–0 lead. Then in round two, Cal scored before Stanford's Kelley O'Hara matched it. Now it was round three, Stanford leading 2–1, and Coach McGuire called on Alex. Cal desperately needed a goal or they risked falling helplessly behind. This was the biggest shot of Alex's career thus far—the one she had worked her life toward—a penalty kick, in a shootout, in a NCAA Tournament, against her team's biggest rival. She proved she could handle the pressure by quickly hitting the back of the net and delivering a goal. It was matched, however, by Christen Press. Stanford still led, 3–2.

In round four, Cal evened it up with a goal and a

save on a Stanford shot. Then it was 4–4. Then it was 5–5. Then it was 6–6. On and on it went, with neither team backing down. This was the most heated and emotional game Alex, or maybe anyone else on the pitch, had ever played. Each team's season dangled in the balance. Finally, in the eighth penalty kick frame, Cal missed and Stanford scored the game winner.

Stanford advanced. A devastated Cal team that had dreamed of a national title was eliminated. Alex was disappointed, but it was a successful season. She started fifteen of the seventeen games she appeared in, led the team with eight goals, and also had ten assists. She'd learned a ton about how to play the game strategically and now understood the amount of effort and determination required at the college level. No one wants to lose, but she was just a freshman. She liked Cal's potential going forward.

Besides, while she didn't know it at that moment, even bigger things were ahead.

5
Under-20

DURING THE SPRING of Alex's freshman year, she was invited to train with the US under-20 women's national soccer team. It was a huge moment.

US Soccer has national teams for players under the age of fifteen, sixteen, seventeen, eighteen, nineteen, twenty, and twenty-three. Then there is the ultimate team, the United States Women's National Team, which is the group that plays in the World Cup and the Olympics. Being on the U-20 team is an important step in reaching the USWNT, which was Alex's main goal. The USWNT will often pull players directly off the U-20. If you prove yourself to be one of the best players on the U-20 team, the path is clear.

When she received her training invite, Alex was just eighteen years old. She was jumping from the U-17 team directly to the U-20. It was clear the national team managers saw her potential, even though she was still recovering from the knee injury during her freshman year at Cal. She was good, but she wasn't as explosive or as fast as she had been in the past.

The training camp was just a few days long, and every minute would be important as Alex was matched up with the best players in the country. Coaches at the camp observe every drill, every possession, every touch of the ball. Practices are even filmed and re-watched later. The pressure is considerable because there is so much at stake.

Alex was happy to discover the training camp was at the StubHub Center in Carson, California, which is located just south of Los Angeles and only about a thirty-mile drive from Diamond Bar. That meant Alex could visit her family while there, offering her a measure of comfort and support.

The StubHub Center felt like home. In 2004, when Alex was just fourteen years old, she and some of her friends went there to watch the USWNT play the "retirement game" for legendary players Mia Hamm, Julie Foudy, and Joy Fawcett. Alex, like millions of other kids, had grown to love the game watching those players win the 1999 World Cup and the 1996 and 2004 Olympics. They were her heroes.

Every time someone plays in a game for the national team, it is said they receive a cap. The term comes from the United Kingdom when, in the 1800s, actual caps or hats were either handed out or worn during competition. Though that tradition ended, the term is still used today to describe the number of games someone has played for a specific team. That night was Hamm's 276th cap and Foudy's 274th. Fawcett didn't play in the game but was honored anyway. She finished her career with 241 caps.

Kristine Lilly, Alex's favorite player growing up, played that night, too. Kristine wouldn't retire until 2010, finishing with 354 career caps—a world record. No one else, female or male, has ever played more games for their national team.

All of those numbers seemed incredible to Alex.

So many games, so many victories, so many goals. Most importantly, though, on that night in 2004, she saw the players sharing a true love of one another and what they had accomplished together—not just on the field, but in serving as role models for a generation of young girls.

"This is more than just being teammates," Foudy, who now works as a soccer broadcaster for ESPN, said that night. "This is a friendship for a lifetime, and that's what has been so special."

Alex watched from the stands and cheered. She also reaffirmed her goal of one day being on the team and having the kind of career and impact that Hamm, Foudy, Lilly, and others did. She promised herself she would do everything she could to make the national team.

Now here was a chance to take a big step in that direction. The U-20 team isn't just the feeder team for the USWNT. U-20 also plays in major international tournaments, such as the FIFA U-20 World Cup. That's where Alex would have the chance to shine on a global stage. She was determined to play well at the camp.

And then she didn't. Her training didn't go well. Maybe it was nerves. Maybe she wasn't ready.

Whatever it was, when they selected the team to compete in the U-20 World Cup, she wasn't on it. Alex tried to remain positive. She was still young, she told herself. There would be other chances. And she had a great team at Cal to concentrate on, of course.

Still, it stung. Everything had happened so fast and then ended just as quickly. It was like when she didn't make the travel club at age thirteen. Was she really good enough? Would she ever be good enough? The doubts were natural.

Then, a few weeks later, a player was taken off the roster. Suddenly there was an opening on the team. Alex got the call. "I was shocked," she said. And thrilled. She called her parents. She called Coach McGuire. Alex would be on the U-20 national team and play in the FIFA U-20 World Cup in Chile in November 2008. The roster included some future friends, including Meghan Klingenberg and Sydney Leroux. It was an incredible opportunity.

Alex spent the rest of the year bouncing between two teams—her college team at Cal and the U-20 national team. The schedule was hectic. She might attend classes and train a couple days with Cal and then jump off for a friendly with the U-20 team in

England. She was anything but your typical college sophomore, although she did everything she could to be a normal teammate.

"She was just one of the girls and spent time with her teammates in the manner all teammates do," Coach McGuire said. "She always had time for the people she cared for."

The real challenge would come during the Cal season. US Soccer training camps and friendlies would cause her to miss some regular-season games. And the actual U-20 World Cup would take place in November, which meant she'd miss the NCAA Tournament—the biggest games of the year for the Bears.

The U-20 team was important, though. Alex wanted to prove she was worthy of her spot on the roster and not just a last-minute replacement who didn't deserve to be there. If that meant missing a couple of Cal games, then that's what would have to happen. Coach McGuire understood. That's how college soccer works. If you want to have elite players on your team, you are going to lose them to US Soccer sometimes. Alex wasn't the only Bear on the U-20 team. Her teammate Megan Jesolva also made it.

"We are blessed at Cal to have many exceptional

players, and when you lose your most talented players it can prove challenging," Coach McGuire said. "However, it is a burden we are glad to have. We will always support our players representing their national teams as there is no greater honor in soccer. Alex missed a great deal, but we always support her in doing so and she was always very respectful of her Cal teammates. She worked hard to balance playing for two teams."

"I put all my effort into my teams, and I take pride in wearing any jersey, Cal or the US," Alex said.

In August, as the Cal season began, Alex was better than ever. She was finally fully recovered from her knee injury, and the U-20 practices had helped her develop as a player. Cal started the season ranked number fifteen in the country. The Bears won five of their first six games, and Alex scored four goals and recorded three assists. Then they took a road trip to Texas and lost twice. Then they began to really struggle and ended the season on a three-game losing streak. They barely made the NCAA Tournament. With Alex and Megan gone, they lost in the first round to the University of Florida, to finish the season with a disappointing 10–9–1.

Meanwhile, Alex was preparing for a momentous occasion on the global stage. To most people, the FIFA U-20 World Cup is not as big of a deal as the regular FIFA Women's World Cup. Only the most die-hard fans follow it. That doesn't mean it is any less competitive to the players. This is the first major international competition for a lot of them. There is national pride at stake. There is the understanding that you may be competing against these other players for years to come. And then there is simply the moniker—the World Cup. It's a dream for everyone.

"I can honestly say that I have never been so proud to wear red, white, and blue," Alex said. "When I stood out there [before the game] singing the national anthem, I really felt honored to wear the US jersey and represent my country."

The U-20 World Cup is, like most international tournaments, set up in two stages. There are sixteen teams that are divided into four groups of four. Each team plays the other three teams in their group, which is called group play. The top two teams in each group advance to the quarterfinals in the knockout stage. Then it is single elimination: Either you win and advance, or you lose and get "knocked out" and go home.

The US went 2–1 in the group stage, with shutout victories over France and Argentina and a loss

54

to China. Alex scored three goals. It was enough to reach the knockout stage where they defeated England 3–0 in the quarterfinals and Germany 1–0 in the semifinals. That was four shutouts—and three relatively lopsided results—in five games. The US was proving they had some of the best young talent in the world, including Alex.

Alex had been wearing a pink headband in games for a few years for a couple of reasons—it helped hold her hair in place, she liked the color pink, and it was a way for her family to easily find her on the field. It took on a different meaning at the U-20 World Cup.

During her freshman year at Cal, she met Servando Carrasco, who played on the Bears men's soccer team. Servando was born in the San Diego area but spent part of his childhood in Mexico, where he became obsessed with the game of soccer. He returned to California for high school and established himself as one of the best players in the state. In 2007, he was also a freshman at Cal. He and Alex became fast friends as they tried to adjust to college life. Within about a month, they began dating. They've been together ever since, and were married in 2014.

In the fall of 2008, Servando's mother, Gloria,

was battling breast cancer. Feeling helpless all the way down in South America, Alex decided the pink headband would honor Gloria and let her know she was thinking of her, because pink is the color associated with breast cancer awareness. Alex grabbed a roll of pink medical wrap. Generally, medical tape is wrapped around someone's ankle before a trainer applies heavier, stickier athletic tape that provides support for an injury or is used as a preventative measure. Instead, Alex pulled off a good-sized piece, tied the ends together, rolled it up, and placed it above her forehead. It was a homemade headband. It's become her signature look and a way to honor women battling breast cancer. "I would never play soccer without my pink headband," Alex says now. Best of all, however, is that Gloria defeated the disease that year.

With her signature headband in place, Alex and her teammates stepped onto the field in the 2008 finals against North Korea, which had won the 2006 U-20 World Cup and had a strong program. The game took place in a stadium tucked in the middle of a crowded neighborhood of Santiago, the capital of Chile. A sell-out crowd of twelve thousand fans came to watch. The atmosphere was exciting. Alex had never played in front of so many wild fans.

The Americans immediately went on the offensive, with Sydney Leroux scoring on a long shot in the twenty-third minute. The North Koreans were undeterred, though, and kept pressing. It was an extremely intense and hard-fought game. Then, in the forty-second minute, Alex would experience a play that would, in many ways, change her soccer career forever.

Since this was the U-20 World Cup championship game, everyone in US Soccer was paying attention. Winning a World Cup at any level is an enormous accomplishment. Any time a player shines in a big, pressure-filled game, she's going to be noticed. The results that follow can often be life changing.

In the stands that day in Santiago was Pia Sundhage, the Swedish-born head coach of the US Women's National Team—the team Alex ultimately wanted to play for and help lead to future World Cup titles. Having the coach you want to play for, watching your game is a huge opportunity.

Just before halftime, Alex received an inbound throw from teammate Elli Reed. Alex was on the right side of the field about forty yards out, and was able to get past the first defender marking her. Two additional North Korean defenders, however, immediately surrounded her. With a lot of speed and a beautiful technical move in which she used her right foot to tap the ball behind her left leg, Alex was able to slip between them and pinch toward the center of the field. As she approached the outside of the penalty area, another defender stepped up in an attempt to stop the play. Alex was now around twenty-five yards out and about to lose control of the ball. She didn't panic, though. She pushed the ball across the field with one touch, gaining just enough space to lay into a heavy shot with her left foot. She hit it so hard the momentum caused her to fall down. It certainly wasn't an ideal way to attack or shoot, but at this level, there is very little time to make plays.

The result was what mattered. The ball soared over the North Korean goalie's outstretched hands before tucking itself into the left upper ninety of the goal, near where the crossbar and goalpost meet. It was the perfect shot, a shot no one could have saved. It came after beating four defenders, showing Alex's skills, speed, and creativity. Her teammates went crazy. This was a world-class goal—one that very few players could attempt, let alone execute.

"That goal in the U-20 World Cup is how Alex

made a name for herself," said Julie Foudy, who has broadcast many of Alex's games on ESPN.

The US would go on to win 2–1. The team jumped around and celebrated as World Cup champions. They had come together as a team and beaten the best in the world. It was emotional. It was exciting. It was one of those moments they'll remember for the rest of their lives. It might have technically been just the U-20 World Cup, but it didn't feel that way to them.

And Alex had given Pia Sundhage plenty to think about for the future.

6

Rising Up

ON THANKSGIVING MORNING 2009, Alex was home in Diamond Bar. She was expecting to enjoy a leisurely day of rest, food, and family. Her Cal season was over. School was out for the long holiday weekend. For one day at least, soccer was the furthest thing from her mind.

Then her phone rang. It was Cheryl Bailey, the general manager of the US Women's National Team.

"Alex, we want you to come train with us," Cheryl said.

Alex couldn't say yes quickly enough. She was only twenty years old and she had been invited to train with the national team. This was the team that would compete in the 2011 World Cup and the 2012 Olympics. This was the team Alex had been dreaming of playing for since she was a little girl. This was, perhaps, the greatest phone call of her life.

A training camp invite didn't assure her a spot on the roster. There would be future cuts. It gave her an opportunity, though, and an opportunity is all that any great competitor wants. Alex was confident that if she played her game and didn't get too nervous, she could make the roster. Immediately after hanging up she went and told her parents, who had spent countless hours driving her to practices and games, nursing her injuries, running through makeshift drills in the backyard, and, maybe most importantly, teaching her to believe in herself. They had sacrificed so much for her. What better way to say thank you than sharing this wonderful news . . . on Thanksgiving Day no less?

It was a welcome bit of positivity after a tough fall soccer season at Cal. Alex entered the 2009 college season hoping for big things out of her team. Unlike in 2008, there were no major US Soccer tournaments or camps, so she could concentrate on college soccer and chasing a national title.

It started well. By mid-September, Cal was 6–1 on the season, ranked number seven in the country. Alex already had seven goals and three assists. The entire team was playing great. Then trouble hit. Megan Jesolva, who also had the U-20 World Cup experience for the US, was injured, robbing Cal's team of one of its most complete players. Trying to find their way, the Bears took on California Polytechnic State University, an opponent they should have beaten handily. Instead Cal Poly upset them, 1–0. A week later, Cal played Sacramento State, another team they should have defeated. Instead Sac State pulled an upset also, 1–0. Making matters worse, Coach McGuire stepped away from the team, citing "personal issues," which didn't go over well with the players, who at the time saw it as their coach quitting.

Alex took to social media to vent. "You turned your back on us once," she tweeted. "We can and will turn our backs on you for good. You are not welcome back." She later said she regretted going public with her personal feelings on a team issue. It was an important lesson about social media. There was now a permanent record of what she said when she was angry in the moment. Her tweet was published in local newspapers.

She vowed to learn from that. Still, there was a lot of confusion. Would Coach McGuire return? There was no time to sort things out, so assistant volunteer coach Kelly Lindsey took over as the interim head coach. Cal played at Santa Clara, the number eleven team in the country, the very next day.

In that game, the Bears showed they still could hang with the best. Alex scored in the first half. Santa Clara came back and the game ended 1–1, but it was a hard-fought performance and a big improvement from the earlier losses to Cal Poly and Sacramento State. Coach McGuire soon returned to the team and apologized for having to step away. It was a temporary issue. The Cal athletic department continued to fully support him. The players may have been angry at first, but he was their coach. It was important to forgive him and get back to being a team.

The reunion started with a road trip sweep of the University of Oregon and Oregon State University, with Alex scoring two goals and adding an assist. But the success was short-lived. The Bears promptly lost four consecutive games, including in-state juggernauts USC and UCLA. In the season finale, they were beat soundly 4–1 by top-ranked Stanford despite a goal from Alex. The Bears managed just three shots. Megan Jesolva returned but she was limited to just forty-two minutes of play time. While they had done enough to reach the NCAA Tournament, they were unranked nationally, with a record of 10–8–1.

In the NCAAs, they defeated Auburn 2–1 in the first round. Alex scored her fourteenth goal of the season. Top-seeded Florida State University was next, and the game was played in Tallahassee, Florida, on FSU's campus. Right out of the gate, the Bears were at a disadvantage with the home crowd rooting against them. Florida State's game plan was simple—stop Alex from even getting the ball, let alone scoring. It worked. She managed just two shots and FSU cruised to a 3–0 victory, ending the Bears' season.

"We really focused on Alex Morgan," Florida State Coach Mark Krikorian said. "When I saw her [against Auburn] I thought she was excellent, just excellent. She is one of the best attacking players that I have seen in the college game."

In soccer, even a top-quality player needs other

top-quality players to succeed. One person can be a difference maker, but no player can singlehandedly carry a team. That is just the reality as the level of competition increases. For Alex to achieve her true potential, she'd need to be surrounded by at least one other player who could make a defense pay if they focused too much on stopping her. Put two players like that together on a soccer pitch, and the goals will come.

Cal didn't have that. The USWNT did.

Abby Wambach was a twenty-nine-year-old veteran when Alex first got invited to train with the national team. A five-foot-eleven forward, Abby hailed from Rochester, New York, and had a knack for scoring goals. Lots and lots of goals. Abby would eventually score more goals—184—in international competition than any player ever, male or female.

Abby and Alex were two different players at two different stages of their careers, but Coach Pia Sundhage believed they could form an amazing tandem in the years to come. Alex was incredibly fast. Abby was incredibly physical—a force in the middle—especially on balls in the air. She was so tall and strong that defenders just bounced off her as she rose and headed shots into the net. If Alex turned out to be as good as Pia thought she could be, there was no way an opposing team could cover both of them.

When she arrived at training camp, Alex tried not to act like she was in awe of Abby, or any of the other players who she had watched, and at times idolized, for years. She instead tried to fit in with her new teammates, such as Carli Lloyd, Megan Rapinoe, Hope Solo, Heather O'Reilly, Shannon Boxx, and others. That behavior especially applied to Kristine Lilly, who was thirty-eight at the time but still going strong. Kristine was Alex's favorite player growing up, and the inspiration for her jersey number choice (13). As a rec player in Diamond Bar, Alex wore number 1. When she started following the sport more closely, she watched the national team and came to respect Kristine's game. That's when she switched to 13, which she wore throughout high school and at Cal. On the national team, Kristine was number 13, so Alex was first given number 21 and later wore number 5. Kristine said when she eventually retired, however, Alex could have the number 13 jersey. It was an incredible honor.

Alex also tried to avoid being intimidated by Pia, who would eventually choose the national team roster. Pia was forty-nine at the time and a soccer legend. She grew up in Sweden, played for their national team at just fifteen years old, and went on to a great career as a professional. Now a coach, she was known for her singular focus on the game. When it came to how soccer should be played, she was a taskmaster.

While Pia was a kind and thoughtful person who liked to lighten the mood by singing to the players, she spent little time trying to get to know their personal lives. She mainly discussed soccer strategy. She had little interest in anything else. As coach of the USWNT she was twice invited to the White House to meet with the president (once with George W. Bush and then with Barack Obama). It's an opportunity most people would jump at. Pia declined. "Showing off and meeting important old men and women doesn't particularly fascinate me," she told a Swedish newspaper. "I'm at my happiest on the pitch in a pair of football shoes." That's Pia. She was a coach. A great coach. She would do everything to get the most out of a player on the field, but that was it.

Alex was perfectly happy with that approach. She wanted to maximize her potential. That magical goal in the U-20 World Cup Final had made an impression on Pia. Now Alex needed to prove it wasn't a fluke. The pressure at the camp was incredible. Everyone there was a great player. The difference between everyone was minuscule. There were also very few spots available. Most of the team was made up of returning stars and proven players, leaving approximately ten spectacularly talented and driven women to battle it out for one or two positions. As such, the littlest thing could make or break someone, which made every rep in every drill matter.

This time Alex was better prepared, though. She just tried to play her game and hoped that it would be enough. That's all anyone could do. Overanalyzing things would just make it worse. Alex also found an unlikely advantage—finals. The camp took place when Cal students were going through their end-of-semester exams. Alex made arrangements with her professors to take them remotely from the camp. As grueling as this sounded, Alex said it actually allowed her to turn off soccer once training ended and not think or worry about anything but the next test she needed to ace. She couldn't control what Pia thought. She could control whether she got good grades on her finals.

Camp went well enough that Alex was invited

back for another session later that winter. That led to her getting invited to play in a March exhibition game against Mexico in Sandy, Utah, a suburb of Salt Lake City. That meant she would officially don a USWNT jersey.

The game was memorable for more than just Alex's first national team appearance—she came on as a sub after halftime. It was also the first time the national team had ever played in the snow. It was late March and spring was officially under way, but that doesn't mean much in the mountains of Utah, as snow fell throughout the game, covering the field with as much as three inches of powder. Since soccer doesn't have time-outs like other sports, there was nothing the stadium crew could do to clean up the field during the match. The snow caused players to slip and slide around. Sometimes the ball skidded faster than expected. Other times it got caught up in a small pile of snow and stopped. Only 3,700 fans watched in the stadium due to the conditions, but they were treated to a game that, if nothing else, was entertaining.

That night in Utah, Alex was nervous about her first game and uncertain about playing in the snow—she was from Southern California after all. Abby was used to it, having grown up in Western

New York, so she told everyone that she had a plan for how to celebrate if the Americans were able to score a goal.

"We were walking out before the game started and I said, 'If anybody scores, snow angels for sure,'" Abby told the local *Deseret News* that night. "And if we got [goal number two] it was going to be a snowball fight."

Just having their star player be that loose helped the entire team. Sure enough, in the sixtieth minute, Abby knocked home a rebound to give the Americans a 1–0 lead. She immediately raced to the right corner of the field, slid down through the powder, and began doing a snow angel, flapping her bare legs and arms in the accumulation. Her teammates, including Alex, had no choice but to do the same, no matter how cold it felt.

"The snow angels were great," Abby told the newspaper. "We, as a team, probably struggle to celebrate well, so I'm proud of us for following through with what we said we were going to do."

No matter how hard the Americans tried, no one scored again. Much to their disappointment, there would be no on-field snowball fight. The US won 1–0, though, and playing for this national team, Alex realized, was going to be a lot of fun.

7

Qualifying

PLAYING IN THE friendly against Mexico in March 2010 only reaffirmed Alex's goal of becoming a national team regular. She had no time to waste. The 2011 FIFA Women's World Cup was set to take place in Germany the following summer. The year after that would be the 2012 Olympics in London. US Soccer might have a rotation of thirty or thirty-five players coming to camps or dressing for exhibition games, but only twenty-one would make the World Cup team. Competition for those final spots is always intense. Alex needed to prove she belonged. It wouldn't be easy. These were the best thirty or so players in America, and it wasn't just her dream to play in a World Cup; it was everyone's dream.

Alex was fitting in with the team, though. The other players saw her potential. "The more I train with the team, the more comfortable I feel," Alex said. "Not only on the field, but off the field, as I get to know my teammates' personalities more." Since she was the youngest player on the team, her teammates teased her like older sisters would. She even earned a nickname—"Baby Horse." The baby part was for being so young. The horse part was playfully making fun of the way she ran, with long strides—like a horse.

"Have you seen her run?" Captain Shannon Boxx laughed at the time. "It's a baby horse. She doesn't like it either, which is why we keep calling her that."

Alex could only smile and accept it. This is what it's like to be the new kid. At least the older players she had idolized were accepting her.

She was just trying to match their level of play in every drill.

"Everyone comes out to practices with one hundred percent intensity all the time," Alex said, noting that it's the only way to prepare for the high level of competition. "At the national team level, there aren't as many areas to exploit as in the college game. Every player deserves to be on the field and it is harder to pick out the weak spots in a team. Also, international games are played at a much faster pace than the college level."

As for Cal, it was going to be another uncertain year, with Alex trying to juggle her schedule between two separate teams, trying to be a leader and build chemistry on one, while trying to prove herself on the other. Each brought their own unique challenges.

One thing Alex was handling well was her academics. Her soccer career had taken off, but Alex never stopped prioritizing the student part of being a student-athlete. In both her sophomore and junior seasons, she was named honorable mention to the conference All-Academic team as well as All-Conference for her play. Alex decided to spend the summer of 2010 taking classes at Cal so she could graduate a semester early. That would free up the spring of 2011 to focus on the women's national team and trying to make the World Cup roster.

Cal started the 2010 season hot. Through eight games, the Bears were 5–0–3 and Alex scored ten goals, the most in the nation at the time. Then she had to depart for the national team and the Bears went on a skid, recording one tie and two losses. When she returned, they won two of three matches and she had four more goals, including her fifth career college hat trick against USC. Then she was gone for the final five games of the regular season. Cal went 2–2–1. The Bears barely managed to qualify for the NCAA Tournament. Alex was the glue that held the team together, and without her they couldn't compete against the best teams in the nation.

The trade-off was the experience Alex gained on the national team, particularly during a friendly against China on October 6 in Chester, Pennsylvania, just outside of Philadelphia. Alex came off the bench in the seventy-first minute with China leading 1–0. About twelve minutes later, with time running out, Abby Wambach chased down a long pass from Heather Mitts just at the top of the penalty area. Abby outfought a defender and flicked the ball with her head over to a charging Alex, who bumped off and raced past her defender. With a beautiful first touch with her left foot, she shot it past the goalkeeper.

Alex jumped for joy, and the first teammate to celebrate with her was none other than Kristine Lilly. Soon Alex was mobbed by everyone, both for evening up a game that would end as a 1–1 tie, and for scoring her first international goal. It was also the first time she and Abby had combined for a score. It was almost exactly how Coach Pia had envisioned it—Abby making a brilliant play to get the ball, and then Alex using her speed and skill to capitalize on it.

That was enough for Alex to make the twenty-player roster to go to Mexico in late October through early November to qualify for the World Cup. Even though the Americans were the top-ranked team in the world at the time and thus a favorite to win the World Cup, they still had to qualify. All teams do.

In soccer, qualifying means proving yourself as one of the best teams in your area of the world. For the United States, that group is the Confederation of North, Central American and Caribbean Association Football (CONCACAF). Each region of the world has something similar—there's the Union of European Football Associations (UEFA), the Asian Football Confederation (AFC), and so on.

The two finalists in the qualifying tournament

would automatically advance to the World Cup. The third-place team would play a team from Europe in a two-game series with the winner qualifying. The United States has played in every FIFA Women's World Cup ever held (1991 was the first). Expectations were high. So was the pressure, even if some of their opponents were overmatched. One loss could change everything.

Alex's participation in the World Cup qualifying tournament was the reason she missed the final five games of Cal's regular season. She was determined to make the most of her time in Mexico. The US cruised through the first three games, winning by a combined score of 18–0. Alex scored once and played well off the bench, providing speed and energy. The Americans were playing like the best team in the world. In the semifinals they faced Mexico, with the winner automatically going to the World Cup. Mexico was a promising team, but a huge underdog to the US. In twenty-five meetings through the years, Mexico had never defeated the Americans. Even though this game would be played in front of a rowdy crowd in Cancun, Mexico, almost everyone expected the US to dominate.

Instead, Mexico stunned them, scoring in the third minute and eventually winning 2–1. It was one of the biggest upsets in women's soccer history. History may have favored the Americans, but on that night, the Mexicans had more energy and execution. It was a reminder that in soccer, anything can happen.

"You can't take anything for granted," Pia said.

The loss left the US reeling. Here Alex thought she just had to prove herself to Pia and she'd play in the World Cup. Now the Americans were on the verge of not even qualifying. No one could believe it. To make it now, they needed to defeat Costa Rica in the third-place game and then win a two-game series in late November against Italy. Anything less and the US would be watching the World Cup on television. A few days after the loss to Mexico, step one was accomplished, a 3–0 victory over Costa Rica. That set the stage for two games against Italy— November 20 in Padua, Italy, and November 27 in Bridgeview, Illinois, outside of Chicago.

First, though, Alex had a week to return to Cal, which was about to head off to the NCAA Tournament. She still hoped to make a run toward the NCAA Championship and wanted one last chance to play with her college teammates. Cal meant a lot to her, and at this point she was one of the finest players in college soccer. She would finish as a top-three finalist for the Hermann Trophy, which goes to the national player of the year.

At first Pia didn't want her to play and risk injury in what were sure to be very intense, physical NCAA Tournament games. But Alex wouldn't stop begging Pia to allow it, and eventually she relented. Alex took the field against Duke University in a round one match-up. Unfortunately for Cal, even with their star player back in the lineup, it wasn't enough. Alex assisted on a goal in the first half to give Cal a 1–0 lead, but Duke quickly responded scoring two goals in a single minute. Duke then held off Cal the rest of the way to win.

Just like that, Alex Morgan's college career was over. She played just twelve games for Cal as a senior but notched fourteen goals. The Bears finished 9–6–5. While Alex didn't achieve her dream of a national title, she left Cal as a proud Bear. She was named All-American as well as once again earning All-Conference, and honorable mention All-Academic honors. She graduated in December, a semester early, with a degree in political economics, which was an incredible accomplishment.

"The University of California is the best public university in the world, where the best and brightest minds graduate in four years," Coach McGuire said.

"To be able to graduate in three and a half years while playing for both Cal and the full women's national team shows how competitive she is."

Alex scored forty-five goals in her collegiate career. She grew as both a player and a person, met her future husband, and despite the drama of her junior season, established a lasting relationship with Coach McGuire, whom she supports and speaks to regularly.

"I wouldn't be who I am if not for my time at Cal," Alex said.

After the NCAA Tournament loss, Alex quickly turned her attention to the national team, which soon flew to Italy. To qualify for the World Cup, the US needed to score more goals than the Italians across the two games. A team could lose 1–0 but then win 3–1 and advance on total goals: 3–2. That put extra pressure on the forwards to score. That pressure grew as the score remained 0–0 deep into the first game. Neither team appeared capable of breaking through. In the eighty-sixth minute, Pia put Alex in, telling her to use her fresh legs and great speed to make something happen against a tiring Italian defense.

"We were waiting and waiting [to put Alex in] and said, 'What the heck, let's do it,'" Pia said after.

In the ninety-fourth minute (four minutes into stoppage time), Alex got her chance. Carli Lloyd sent a long pass across midfield to about the thirty-yard line, where Abby Wambach headed it forward, through two Italian defenders and into some open space at the top of the box. That's where a charging Alex flew into the action. The Italian defenders were exhausted and unable to keep up. Alex took two touches and then from six yards out drilled a shot past the goalkeeper.

Gooooaaaalllllll, USA!

Alex turned and jumped for joy and eventually into Abby's arms. The Italians were stunned. The Americans were thrilled. They would return to America with a one-goal lead and the inside track on the World Cup bid. It meant they could play for a tie in the second game and still advance because of total goals. Tactically, it was a huge advantage.

In the second match, they won 1–0 anyway to qualify. Alex's goal, her fourth in eight appearances with the national team in 2010, was considered the key.

When Pia eventually announced the World Cup roster that would go to Germany, Alex Morgan was on it.

8

2011 World Cup

THE WORLD CUP began in late June 2011. Before then, Alex achieved another childhood dream, one she first declared in a note to her mother back when she was eight: She became a professional soccer player. Women's Professional Soccer (WPS) was the pro league in the United States at the time. In January, they held their annual draft of college players. Since Alex graduated a semester early, she was eligible. Unlike at college, where players are recruited and get to choose where they want to go, in professional sports each team takes turns picking which players they want.

Alex was the first overall pick, selected by the Western New York Flash, which was based out of Rochester. It was quite an honor. A couple of Alex's future USWNT teammates, Meghan Klingenberg (University of North Carolina) and Christen Press (Stanford) went third and fourth overall. The Flash was an expansion team, meaning they were a new addition to the league, but they had some talent, including Alex's fellow national team member Yael Averbuch, plus two sensational international players, Christine Sinclair from Canada and Marta Vieira da Silva from Brazil, who is called "Marta" because in Brazil, the best players are known solely by their first names. As one of the all-time greatest players, Marta certainly deserves the distinction. The downside for Alex? She needed to report to cold, snowy Rochester to begin training, which was quite a change for a California native.

"Learning how to dress for the cold was much different," Alex joked.

If Alex had thought temporarily jumping back and forth between Cal and the USWNT was tough, the time had come for her to accept that such a lifestyle would be her full-time reality. Naturally, players in the WPS earned a salary, but they also had obligations to their respective national teams, which paid them to play, too. More importantly, the national team offered the exposure necessary to earn endorsement money and appear in commercials. None of the contracts were big compared to the best players in men's soccer, let alone players in the National Basketball Association or Major League Baseball. Only the best female soccer players were making over $100,000 a year by combining their pay for their professional team and the national team. An NBA player could make $30 million a season. Same with great male soccer players such as Cristiano Ronaldo or Lionel Messi, who make even more. Women were (and still are) paid much less than men, and while some of that is due to lower attendance and television ratings, it remains frustrating. The US Women's National Team is far more successful than the US Men's National Team.

Years later, Alex would be part of a movement demanding equal pay that got the US Women's National Team to up their players' salaries. That was in the future. Right now, the money she was earning wouldn't make her rich, but it was at least something.

Alex and the others were making a living playing soccer, a game they loved. If that meant constantly bouncing to and from USWNT and the WPS, then that's what they would do.

As the 2011 FIFA Women's World Cup began, there was a buzz among fans and media about Alex. She was the youngest player on the team, set to turn twenty-one in the middle of the tournament. Despite her inexperience, she had already delivered some memorable, late-game goals.

"Going into that World Cup, people were like, 'Who is this kid coming off the bench?'" said Julie Foudy, a USWNT legend.

Even if Alex was still developing, her fast-paced style was exciting to watch.

"It always helps that [she has] speed," Foudy said. "She's got this wonderful ability, like any great forward does, where you don't need a ton of looks but can finish. She's tough as nails. Fighting through things, fighting for balls defensively, fighting for balls offensively. And then she's good technically. A lot of young players have the speed but maybe not the technical side of it. Her best asset is that you just know in big moments she is going to deliver. You want her on the field."

The debate among fans and media was whether Alex deserved to start. Yet it wasn't that simple. First off, Alex was playing behind Amy Rodriguez, who was a terrific player in her own right and had been with the national team since the 2008 Olympics. On a team this good, no one just walks in and takes a starting job. Second, Pia believed Alex was having late game success because she was coming in fresh and given a simple job—charge the ball and the goal at all costs. Alex had a role. She needed to keep doing it. Pia had a saying about the importance of the subs—"The team is twenty-one players." It means everyone is of equal importance. If Alex played a full ninety minutes, her job would change. And Alex wasn't ready for that . . . yet.

"If she starts, you can't just tell her to go to goal—it's more complicated than that," Pia explained to the media at the time. "When she has just a couple of minutes, that's different. And she's played her role very well. Eventually she will earn a spot, but right now she's doing well coming off the bench."

Alex would have preferred to start and play the entire game, but she understood. Patience is needed, even if it can be frustrating. She was an up-and-comer on a star-studded team, not the team leader she'd been in college or while playing travel soccer. By not starting her, Pia was also allowing Alex to develop over time. As a result, Alex wasn't burdened with undue attention, which can overwhelm young players.

"I was actually glad Pia didn't start her, and waited," Foudy said. "She kind of tempered the expectations instead of creating a ton of hype."

With her role established, Alex geared up for the opening match. The World Cup was played in two stages—group play and then the knockout stage. The US went 2–1 in their group, defeating North Korea and Colombia, but losing to Sweden. Alex played in two games but didn't score. Losing to Sweden was disappointing, but the US still came in second in their group. That was enough to advance to the quarterfinals to play Brazil and Alex's new Western New York Flash teammate Marta, the five-time FIFA World Player of the Year.

The game was played in Dresden, Germany, in front of a huge crowd and a wild atmosphere. Soccer is extremely popular in Germany and the fans came out to see a great game, even if it featured two nonlocal countries. Players dream of competing in front of crowds like this. The game didn't disappoint.

The US struck first, scoring a goal in the opening minutes, but then in the sixty-eighth minute, American Rachel Buehler fouled Marta in the penalty box just as Marta was about to score. It was an obvious foul and the ref gave Buehler a red card, which meant Marta would get a penalty kick but also that Buehler was thrown out of the game. Even worse, you can't replace a player that is given a red card. The US was forced to play with just ten players the rest of the game. Brazil still had eleven. Not only did that give Brazil an immediate advantage, but the situation would only worsen over the long course of a game. Playing with just ten women on the field can wear out the team since everyone has to expend more energy covering more ground. The pressure was on after Marta evened the game by scoring on the penalty kick.

Alex got into the game and made a number of late runs but couldn't score. In extra time, Marta scored again and Brazil looked like it was about to spring the upset. Then, in the 122nd minute—extra time in overtime—just seconds from being eliminated from the World Cup, Megan Rapinoe did what Megan Rapinoe does—she sent a long, high cross to the back post. That's where Abby Wambach did what Abby Wambach does—she outleaped a defender and the goalie to head in the game-tying goal.

"[It was] the perfect ball," Wambach said, giving credit to Rapinoe.

It was one of the most spectacular goals in women's national team history. Moments later the game went to penalty kicks. One team would leave this game with their hopes for a World Cup title still alive. The other would head home, forced to wait four long years for another shot.

Alex didn't get a chance to shoot, but she watched with bated breath from the sideline. A few minutes later, she celebrated alongside her teammates when the US won 5–3. American goalie Hope Solo was incredible during the PKs, blocking two attempts, and the US survived to play another day.

In the semifinal against France, Alex entered the game in the fifty-sixth minute, just after France tied the game at 1–1. In the seventy-ninth minute, Abby headed one in off a high corner kick to the back post to give the US a 2–1 lead. Then, three minutes later, with France reeling, Abby headed the ball just inside midfield to Megan Rapinoe, who made a single stab of a pass to send the ball through the defense and into open space.

Alex knew what her job was then. She chased down the ball and took two touches to push it to the left side of the box and away from the chasing defenders. It's not often a player has time for two dribbles at that level of play: "I was freaking out by taking an extra touch," Alex said. It ended up working to her advantage. The move drew the French goalkeeper out and left room behind her to pop a shot into the net. "The goalie went low, so I tried to chip it over her," Alex said. It worked.

The goal secured the 3–1 victory and sent the Americans to the finals to play Japan. In doing so, Alex showed poise and patience in a huge moment to score her first World Cup goal.

"Mark my words," Abby said after. "That's the first of many [goals] Alex is going to score in the World Cup."

The 2011 FIFA Women's World Cup Final against Japan was played in Frankfurt, Germany, and even the veteran players were nervous. The game would be played in a historic stadium, Waldstadion (translated as "forest stadium"), which was built in 1925 in the woods just outside Frankfurt. A sell-out crowd of over forty-eight thousand would be there, including many Americans who traveled to watch the game.

There is no greater pinnacle for a soccer player than competing in the World Cup Final. Soccer is played all over the world—in big fields and tight streets, in organized clubs and neighborhood pick-up games. It's the world's game. Almost everyone on Earth has at least kicked a soccer ball or played the game at some level, even if it was just as a little kid. To be one of the forty-two players (twenty-one on each team) to reach this game was an amazing accomplishment. Alex was thinking back to those simple rec games in Diamond Bar, running through drills with her dad, or just hoping to make a travel team. Every player on both teams was thinking of the long journey they'd taken to find their way onto this field. Each of them wanted to be one of the twenty-one who would win it.

Most of the American players came of age watching the 1999 team win the World Cup in Pasadena, California. That was twelve long years ago. It was time for this generation to prove itself.

Waiting in the final was Japan, a team the Americans had a 22–0–3 lifetime record against.

But this was a different Japanese team. They were technically and tactically sound, and they were playing with incredible emotion. Months earlier a major earthquake hit Japan, causing more than fifteen thousand deaths, many more injuries, and incredible damage. The women's team had become a rallying cry and much-needed distraction for the country. Like the US, the Japanese were on an incredible run, upsetting Germany in the quarters despite the game taking place in Germany, and then besting the Swedish team that had beaten the US in group play.

Alex did not start and neither team scored in a tense first half. The United States had more opportunities, including a beautiful shot by Abby that hit the crossbar, but it couldn't break through. Alex came on at halftime and just three minutes later, watched as Heather O'Reilly crossed a ball a few yards in front of the front post. Alex made a quick charge to it, beating the defender and the goalie who was coming out of the box. Alex only had time to jab her right foot on the ball as she slid down. It got past the defender but ricocheted off the goalpost. Japan harmlessly cleared the rebound away. It was *so* close.

Then came the sixty-ninth minute. Japan was on

the attack before Megan Rapinoe collected a ball just on top of the American box. She took two touches and then saw Alex deep on the other side of the field. There were three Japanese defenders back, but there was also some space to send a ball, so Megan did, launching it fifty yards. Alex charged after it, gaining position on the defender marking her.

The ball bounced once, then twice, and Alex got a touch on it with her right boot just at the top of the penalty area to control it. Still in full stride, and with no time or space to spare, she blasted the ball with her left foot from about sixteen yards. The ball ripped past the diving goalie, hitting the inside panel of the right side of the net. It was a brilliant play from start to finish. Alex Morgan had scored a World Cup Final goal and the US held a 1–0 second half lead.

The game wasn't over, though. Japan, which had barely threatened to score all day, went all out and netted an equalizer in the eightieth minute.

The game went to extra sessions tied 1–1 when Alex collected a ball on the right flank, down near the end line. Alex had a poor angle to shoot from but spied Abby set up perfectly in front of the net. Alex made a quick skill move to gain space and crossed the ball to the front of the net to Abby who headed it in with authority to get the 2–1 lead.

Alex became the first player to ever score a goal and record an assist in a World Cup Finals. That was the last thing on her mind, though. Preserving the victory was all that mattered.

The US couldn't do it. Japan wouldn't be denied and scored in the 117th minute, just a few moments before the end of extra time. At 2–2, the game went to penalty kicks where Japan won, 3–1. Alex didn't get called on to shoot. A game that appeared won, was lost. No one could believe it.

"When I scored that goal, I thought we were winning," Alex said. "Then the momentum shifted and they came back and scored again. Once we went into penalties, they had all the momentum with them. It went from almost perfect to the worst day that we could ever imagine."

"There is a small difference between winning and losing," Pia said.

In the moment, all the Americans could do was vow that next time they would find that small difference.

9

London

AS DISAPPOINTED AS Alex and her teammates were over losing the World Cup, they didn't want to do or say anything that might be seen as a slight against Japan. Yes, the Americans thought they should have won, but they didn't. Managing to be upset about a loss without taking anything away from the other team's joy is important. That's good sportsmanship and, as much as anything, that is a value the US women wanted to convey. You have to handle losing with the same class that you display when you win.

"It is something we were taught from a young age," Alex said, "because we respect every international women's team at such a high level. We respect the women for making the journey. Sportsmanship is important in our sport because they fought just as much to get to where they are. I think it's important to shake hands after the game. I think it's important to shake the referee's hand. It's just part of sports in general. Winning is what drives all athletes but it is not what defines us."

Even though they lost, the players were greeted in the United States with incredible support. Their World Cup run had captured the nation's imagination, drawing high television ratings and huge outdoor watch parties in major cities. President Obama, First Lady Michelle, and their two daughters became dedicated fans. A whopping 13.5 million people tuned into the game against Japan—a record at the time for both soccer and women's sports in America. That's more viewers than any game of the 2011 NBA Finals. As a result, everywhere the players went, they found their popularity and fame had soared, despite coming up short.

"I was shocked by how well we were received," Alex said. "Our hearts were broken. We thought we were coming back defeated, but the whole country lifted us when we needed it."

Alex herself had become a star. She was young, talented, and had scored a number of memorable goals. She was also photogenic with a likeable personality. Everyone could see she was one of the future faces of women's soccer. The team itself looked to be on an upswing again, and would be back in the spotlight at the 2012 London Olympics. Over the next few years Alex would sign endorsement deals with Nike, Coca-Cola, U.S. Bank, McDonald's, Chobani yogurt, AT&T, Procter & Gamble, Panasonic, and others. She even appeared in the *Sports Illustrated* swimsuit edition. She was suddenly earning far more money doing advertisements than playing soccer.

However, despite her meteoric rise, as the 2012 women's national team season began, Alex was neither a starter nor, technically, a professional player any longer. In January, the WPS went out of business. It was mismanaged and losing money, so no one was too surprised, but it was a disappointment. Alex's Western New York Flash had won the 2011 championship, beating Philadelphia in penalty kicks. There was a good crowd that day, but the game was probably best remembered for a squirrel that ran onto the field and wouldn't leave, delaying the game. The grounds crew struggled to catch it before finally putting a cardboard box over it and slowly dragging it off the field. It was a funny moment and good for tons of views on YouTube, but the fact that a squirrel overshadowed an exciting championship game probably spelled doom for the league.

As for the national team, Pia kept bringing Alex off the bench during friendlies and Olympic qualifying games (much like the World Cup, you have to qualify for the Olympics). In the first four games of the qualifying tournament, the US won by a combined score of 34–0. The Americans were incredible and the competition was not.

In a 14–0 victory over the Dominican Republic, American Amy Rodriguez scored five times. Then in a 13–0 victory over Guatemala, Sydney Leroux scored five.

Alex had only scored twice heading into the final against Canada, but her play was so strong that Pia finally put her in the starting lineup. It was another dream achieved. She was now expected to be a ninety-minute player, not just a speedster coming in late. Alex responded by scoring twice, including once in the fourth minute, in an eventual 4–0 victory over Canada. The US qualified for the Olympics by outscoring its opponents 38–0. They were the clear gold medal favorite.

Particularly exciting was the on-field chemistry that Alex and Abby were developing. If one wasn't scoring, the other was. Abby also had two goals in the victory over Canada. They not only played well together, often assisting on the other's goals, they challenged defenses just by being out there. They played different styles and defenders didn't know how to react.

In a tournament in Portugal, Alex had five goals and Abby three. In the Swedish Invitational, they each netted three. By the time the London Olympics began, Abby had pulled Alex aside and told her that for the first time since the all-time great Mia Hamm retired in 2004, she felt like she had "a partner in crime" up front, a true connection with someone who could maximize both of their play. Alex, just twenty-three years old and a freshly minted starter, couldn't believe what she was hearing. "Mia Hamm is a legend," she said.

"In my opinion, no one can defend against both of us for a ninety-minute period of time," Abby said. "I like to think of Alex as kind of the kid that has the world in front of her and is literally running at it with every step she takes, every shot she takes, every goal she scores."

Meanwhile, after all her growth as a player, Alex even phased out of her rookie year nickname "Baby Horse." She'd proven herself by then, so her teammates began calling her "Ali" or "Ali Cat" or just "Alex."

"Now she's a beautiful stallion," Rapinoe joked. "I think in the beginning, people may have seen her as a pretty face who scored goals. She is much more than that. Her game has developed so much in the last year. Her future is super bright. She's definitely a superstar."

For all the positive feeling, though, for all the talk about superstars and Mia Hamm, Abby reminded Alex and the rest of the team of one simple thing: "You've got to win to be legends." Abby was on the 2004 Olympic team that took gold. This 2011–2012 team hadn't won anything yet.

The Olympics were set up like the World Cup, a three-game group stage and then a knockout round starting with the quarterfinals. The games were staged all across the United Kingdom—England,

Scotland, and Wales. The Americans were disappointed that they didn't get to march in the opening ceremonies in London, which is a dream of nearly all athletes. Instead they were in Glasgow, Scotland, with a game the next day. The team dressed up anyway and paraded around their hotel when the Americans were introduced. It was the next best thing.

The US rolled through group play, going 3–0. Alex had two goals. Abby had three. The US then defeated New Zealand 2–0 in the quarterfinals.

Then came the epic 4–3 overtime game against Canada in the semifinals in Manchester, England. It was the most hard-fought and intense game Alex had ever played in. The Canadians believed they could win, but the US wouldn't stop fighting either. The game is best known for the clutch, game-winning goal Alex scored in the 123rd minute that cemented her as a USWNT hero. (Remember that epic moment in chapter 1?)

"Some players have a gift of scoring goals when it's most needed," Coach Pia said of Alex. "She has that gift."

In fact, there were a few memorable moments in that game. The Americans' first goal came when Megan Rapinoe hit a corner kick that curled around the front post and went into the net without touching anyone until it was over the line. It counted as a goal. Scoring in such a manner is rare and, coincidentally, called an "Olympic Goal." It requires either putting a lot of spin on the ball or a big wind. In this case, it was probably a combination of both. Rapinoe's was, and remains, the only "Olympic Goal" ever scored during an actual Olympics.

Then there was a game-changing act by Abby, although it was not something she did athletically. Canada led 3–2 late in regulation and was trying to waste time on the clock to get the victory. Stalling is a common tactic for teams in the lead. Sometimes they just kick the ball far out of bounds. In this case, Canadian goalie Erin McLeod kept holding the ball as long as she could before punting it. Abby, however, being the leader she was, knew the rule called for a goalie to get rid of a ball within six seconds of securing it. Anything longer is a penalty, resulting in an indirect penalty kick from wherever the goalie held the ball, which has to be inside the penalty area.

Each time McLeod got possession, Abby began counting out the seconds that she held on to the ball: "One, two . . . eight, nine, ten." She made sure the ref, Christiana Pedersen, heard it.

Pedersen didn't call a penalty at first, but each time Abby did it, it became harder for the ref to ignore. Sometimes, Abby said, she reached the teens before McLeod kicked it away.

"I wasn't yelling. I was just counting," Abby said. "Probably did it five to seven times."

Finally, in the seventy-seventh minute, McLeod got the ball again and Abby began counting. When she reached ten and McLeod still had the ball, the ref blew the whistle for delay of game and awarded the US the indirect kick. The Canadians couldn't believe it. This was a tough, if accurate, call at that point in such an important game. The indirect kick led to a handball, which then led to a penalty kick that Abby knocked home to tie the score. Just like that, it was 3–3.

"We feel like we got robbed," McLeod said after, even though replays showed she held the ball for at least thirteen seconds before the whistle. Later Alex would score the game winner and push the Americans to the gold medal game. It was a reminder that a great player such as Abby can impact a game in many ways.

"Yes, it's uncharacteristic," Abby said. "But the rules are the rules. You can say it's gamesmanship, you can say it's smart, but I'm a competitor. We needed to get a goal. They're trying to waste time; I'm trying to speed it up."

Maybe this is what Pia meant about the "small difference between winning and losing." By finding this difference against Canada, and winning by the slimmest of margins, the Americans were off to London's Wembley Stadium where waiting for them was . . . Japan.

The US didn't need revenge to motivate them in this game. A gold medal was at stake. Plus, there were eighty thousand fans in attendance—the largest crowd to ever watch Olympic women's soccer, and the largest crowd the US had ever played in front of outside America. It was a wild, festive scene and the fans wouldn't have to wait long for some action. Eight minutes in, Carli Lloyd scored on a cross from Alex.

Japan wouldn't go down without a fight, though, and put together a relentless barrage the rest of the half. The US was on its heels, unable to control the ball. That left everyone, even a forward such as Alex, concentrating on defense when she wanted to be looking to score. But despite multiple close calls on goal, the US defense, anchored by goalie Hope

Solo's spectacular performance, held Japan scoreless in the first half.

Carli scored again in the second half on a nice individual run, and then Japan threw everything they had at the Americans. Japan earned one back in the sixty-third minute but never could level the game—Hope made numerous incredible saves. This time the US held on, winning the gold medal and achieving lifelong dreams.

Alex was a champion at last.

"It was amazing," Alex said. "Our team just battled through to the end. We were such a unit and we leaned on each other when we needed to. We're just so happy now. It was such a journey. It was so emotional. We all did it together."

10

Triumph

AFTER THE OLYMPICS, Alex was no longer just a soccer star. She was a breakthrough, mainstream celebrity even to people who barely watched soccer. The national team had become a sensation. As big as the 2011 World Cup was, the 2012 Olympics were even bigger. To capitalize on it, the US team toured America later that summer to celebrate their victory and play friendlies in front of their fans. By the end of the year, Alex had scored twenty-eight goals for the team—a huge number—and found adoring crowds wherever she went.

Almost everything Alex touched became a success. Her endorsement opportunities and media appearances grew by the day. She wrote a bestselling series of books called The Kicks about a fictional middle school soccer team. Alex Morgan merchandise flew off the shelves, including posters, Fatheads wall art, and of course, Alex's now famous number 13 jersey (Kristine Lilly handed over the jersey number in 2010). On social media, Alex's followers on Instagram and Twitter soared. She later published an autobiography, and in 2018 even starred (as herself) in a popular family soccer movie, *Alex and Me*. Her pay, mostly thanks to endorsement and business endeavors, shot up to an estimated $3 million per year—by far the highest among American female soccer players.

One thing Alex and her teammates wanted to do with their newfound fame was to help another women's professional league launch and, this time, actually last. In 2013, the National Women's Soccer League (NWSL) began, featuring eight teams across the country. A television deal was also reached, putting games on ESPN and Fox Sports. The US, Canadian, and Mexican soccer federations all offered financial support because it would help everyone to have their best players in a North American pro league. Maximum pay was just $30,000—a small fraction of what men's professional athletes make—but it was at least something.

Alex was assigned to the Portland Thorns in Oregon. One of her teammates was, again, Christine Sinclair, the Canadian star from that bitter game in London. The pro league was filled with strange relationships like that—rivals became teammates and teammates became rivals.

That first year Portland played the Western New York Flash (which had moved to the NWSL from the failed WPS) for the championship. The Flash wasn't just Alex's old WPS team; its star player was now Abby Wambach. No matter—they battled as hard as ever, and Alex and the Thorns won 2–0 to take the first NWSL championship.

As for the national team, 2013 and 2014 were full of less prestigious tournaments, such as the Algarve Cup in Portugal. While the team played hard and won enough to preserve their number one ranking, it was different this time for Alex. She no longer needed to prove herself worthy of a spot on the team. She was an established leader who worked to help younger players develop for the benefit of the team.

"Alex is a superstar," Julie Foudy, the ESPN

broadcaster, said. "There is more to a team than just the superstar, though. The thing a lot of young players miss is they see a superstar and they think, 'Well I am not a superstar, so I can't be successful at this level.' But what I think is more important is that you are a great teammate. Because people are so focused on goals and results. People don't hear about it, but Alex is awesome in terms of team chemistry and positivity and mentoring other players and helping other players.

"You don't need to be a superstar to do any of that and I think that is something that a lot of young kids miss," Foudy continued. "They aren't the ones scoring all the goals or wearing the captain arm band. They get discouraged. I would argue that they are the most important players because of the attitude they bring. A team can't succeed without that attitude, no matter how good the superstar is."

As Alex rose through the elite rungs of pro soccer, she faced a challenge that all ambitious players deal with—balancing competition with teammates for roster spots and playing time while also remaining supportive and creating a positive team environment. It's like that on every team. How do you fight for playing time in each practice but remain a good teammate? The teams that can work together through tryouts, camps, and practices tend to win.

"That is something that growing up I didn't handle so well, as I'm sure most teenage girls don't handle well," Alex said. "I think our natural instincts are to be competitive with one another because at the very core we are competing for spots on the field. On any team there are going to be players going to the bench, players that are starting, and players that are not going to make the team. It has to be more about the bigger picture."

While Alex was emerging as a core part of the USWNT, change was on the horizon. Pia had announced she was stepping down as coach in late 2012 and would be taking over the Swedish National Team. It was always her goal to return to her homeland and run the program. Alex was surprised, but happy for her. Tom Sermanni took over. He was Scottish and had a strong soccer background, but the team struggled under his leadership. It didn't help that Alex missed numerous games due to an ankle injury. When they finished seventh at the 2014 Algarve Cup (with no Alex)—the worst ever for the US in that event—he was fired.

Jill Ellis was his replacement. Jill was born in

England but moved to the United States as a girl and played at the College of William & Mary in Virginia. She had been the longtime coach at UCLA and worked in development for US Soccer. Jill was different from Pia. They were both competitive and tactically smart, but Jill also valued relationships with her players, helping them through hard times and connecting with them on a personal level. She was about more than just soccer. She regularly scheduled one-on-one meetings with players just to talk. The most common word used to describe her is "nice." She was also a forward-thinking coach, believing in advanced statistics, video analysis, and using technology to gain an edge.

The US qualified for the 2015 FIFA Women's World Cup fairly easily, but it wasn't easy for Alex. She reinjured her left ankle in one game and had to miss most of the action. The highlight of 2014 for Alex was when she and Servando were married during a beach ceremony in Santa Barbara, California. A number of Alex's teammates on the national team attended. Alex and Servando had been together since their freshman year at Cal when they met as promising young soccer players. Even though they often lived in different cities and were constantly traveling due to soccer (Servando was now a pro player as well), they remained together. "I truly married my best friend," Alex said.

It was an otherwise frustrating time for Alex. Just as her ankle healed and she began scoring goals again, she injured her left knee in a NWSL game. Officially it was a contusion, or a bruise, but it was limiting. The World Cup began in late June, and throughout the spring she was still rehabbing. Alex kept fretting about how slowly the contusion was healing. She had waited four years to get another chance at the World Cup, and now she feared missing it.

"The recovery process was taking longer than expected," Alex said, "and I was getting into my own mind and thinking and analyzing too much."

Alex trained as hard as she could once she joined the team in Canada for the World Cup. Jill vowed not to play her until she was 100 percent. There was no need to risk injury until the more crucial games later in the tournament. The US managed fine without her, advancing out of group play to set up a Round of 16 game against Colombia, the first must-win game of the tournament. It was played in Edmonton, Canada, and while the US was the heavy favorite, they knew anything could happen and the dream of a championship could end in ninety minutes. So Alex Morgan would play.

With the score tied 0–0 in the second half, nerves began to tense up. The US was getting chances, but not finishing. An Abby goal was disallowed due to an offside call. Another Abby shot was batted away in a great save. Lauren Holiday and Megan Rapinoe each received yellow cards for physical play. Alex had a breakaway but was tripped up inside the box, causing her to fall hard. A penalty kick was awarded. Abby took it only to uncharacteristically miss the entire frame.

It was shaping up to be that kind of game when nothing goes right when Alex got the ball on the right side in the fifty-third minute. She had a bad angle on the net when she spied the goalie moving toward the middle and out of position. "I was going to cross it but then I saw her give up the near post," Alex said. She took a touch and unloaded a shot with her right foot. The goalie, perhaps surprised that Alex shot rather than passed, managed to get only one hand on it. The ball had enough force to power through and into the net! The US led 1–0 and order was restored. "We needed that breakthrough at the moment," Alex said. The Americans would win 2–0, with Carli Lloyd scoring later on a penalty kick.

The US beat China 1–0 on another Carli goal in the quarterfinals and then took out Germany 2–0 in a tense semifinal game in Montreal. Alex didn't score, but her play was strong. After a frustrating recovery period, she was back at just the right time. Besides, Carli's stellar play was off the charts.

The US headed to the World Cup Final again, four years after the disappointment of blowing a late lead to Japan. And once again, Japan would be their opponent—this time at a sold-out BC Place Stadium in Vancouver. The location was great for the US, since Vancouver sits nearly on the US-Canada border and is only a two-and-a-half-hour drive from Seattle. So many Americans came decked out in red, white, and blue that it looked like a home game.

"It feels incredibly different yet eerily similar, too," Alex said at the time. "We're back playing Japan in the final and we specifically remember [2011] but at the same time, everything is different. We have so many other players stepping up and making big plays. We have a different coach. We are in a different place right now.

"As Abby has said, 'We haven't accomplished

anything,'" Alex continued. "We know we are on the verge of something amazing. We have the world in our hands to continue to grow the game in our country and bring home the first World Cup since sixteen years ago. We were on the verge of that four years ago, though. And it didn't happen."

America was certainly ready for victory. Across this World Cup, the interest in the team and the television ratings for the games just grew and grew. For the first time since the US hosted the 1999 World Cup, the most important USWNT games were being played in North America, and thus televised during primetime or weekend afternoons, not in the middle of the night due to unfriendly time zones. An estimated 8.4 million viewers tuned in for the thrilling semifinal against Germany.

The finals had become a true national event and were scheduled for Sunday, July 5, which was part of a long holiday weekend. Families gathered around televisions. People had neighborhood cookouts to watch. Giant screens were set up in big cities and small towns across the country. The women's national team was America's team, and this game would become the most-watched soccer telecast in United States history, drawing an astounding 26.7

million viewers. That's more viewers than any game of the MLB World Series, NBA Finals, NHL Stanley Cup Final, or college football that season.

It turns out the Americans were going to make sure those tuning in were treated to a world-class performance. There would be no slow start this time, no allowing Japan to hang around and gain confidence, no giving their opponent a chance to come back late. In the third minute, Megan Rapinoe sent a corner kick low into the box, where Carli perfectly timed her run to meet it and, with the outside of her foot, slammed it into the net. It was a set piece designed by Jill, and it was perfectly executed. The US was up 1–0. The crowd at BC Stadium went wild!

Just two minutes later, Lauren Holiday took a free kick on the right side of the Japanese net, almost like a corner. She hit the ball through, and Julie Johnston tipped it up in the air right to Carli who knocked it in. The US was up 2–0. BC Stadium went even wilder.

In the fourteenth minute, Tobin Heath sent a long volley to Alex, who was charging into the penalty area. The pass was deflected by a Japanese defender. The ball popped straight up in the air, and when it came down Lauren Holiday one-timed it for a goal. The US was up 3–0. BC Stadium went even wilder still.

Then, just two minutes later, in the sixteenth minute of the game, Carli got the ball near midfield. Alex was streaking down the right side. The Japanese goalie—and everyone watching—expected Carli to kick the ball into space for Alex to chase down for a scoring attempt. In an effort to prevent that, the goalie began charging out of her box. It was a good anticipatory play except Carli saw it happening and decided to hammer a ball from the center field line—fifty full yards—to the goal. It soared high and long. The goalkeeper stumbled as she tried to retreat, and the ball sailed into the net! It was one of the most spectacular goals in soccer history: a half-court shot. Carli already had a hat trick, the fastest in World Cup history.

The US led 4–0 and the game had barely just begun.

Back at the White House, President Obama was watching and said he couldn't believe the game he had been looking forward to witnessing was essentially decided so quickly.

"I had gotten my popcorn," Obama would tell

the team later. "I was just settling in. I'm thinking I've got a couple hours of tension and excitement. And poof, it was gone. It was over."

The game would end 5–2, Japan playing hard but incapable of overcoming that early avalanche. For the first time in sixteen years, since the days when legendary players like Mia Hamm and Kristine Lilly had helped put US Soccer on the map, the Americans were World Cup champions.

For Alex, this wasn't a World Cup where she racked up tons of goals, but she had battled back from injury and played an enormous role in winning the title. Besides, this was a new era of the national team; it was loaded with record-breaking talent.

"I feel like it all worked out perfectly," Alex said. "I'm just unbelievably proud."

11

Superstar

ALEX DIDN'T HAVE much downtime to celebrate the World Cup. A victory tour was scheduled—a series of friendlies that brought the team across the country to play in front of large crowds of adoring fans—to Pittsburgh, Detroit, Birmingham, San Antonio, and more. There were media demands. There was a ticker tape parade in New York City, where the team rode through lower Manhattan as cut-up paper fell on them like confetti. Alex appeared on *American Idol*, *The Simpsons*, and the

ESPY Awards. There was a visit to the White House to meet President Obama, the self-described "First Fan." His daughter Sasha had even attended the final in Vancouver.

"They've inspired millions of girls to dream bigger," President Obama said. "And by the way, [they] inspired millions of boys to look at girls differently, which is just as important. This team taught all America's children that 'playing like a girl' means [being the best]."

Change was in the air. The World Cup victory had a profound impact in America, highlighted by the increased acceptance the women's game was receiving. A milestone came when Alex was picked to appear alongside Lionel Messi of Argentina on the cover of the EA Sports *FIFA 16* video games sold in the United States. It is annually one of the top-selling games in the country. Not only was Alex on the cover, she was finally "in the game." It was the first edition that featured women's teams as well as men's teams.

"It is an incredible honor," Alex said. "I know people all over the world play this game. I'm really excited [it] is putting such an important spotlight on women's soccer."

Alex began working with the "Like a Girl"

campaign, which encourages girls around the world to participate in sports in an effort to build self-esteem and encourage teamwork among women.

"The Like a Girl campaign is very authentic to me because every girl faces barriers and discouraging people along the way," Alex said. "I faced that when I was younger, and I face that today. It is so important to keep playing, and to feel confident, and to feel encouraged because I want girls to feel the same as I do. It's about showing girls from a young age to believe in themselves. Women are great."

None of the success surprised her old coaches. Kemp Wells, her high school coach, always assumed Alex was destined for greatness "because of her talent and her drive to improve." And Coach McGuire from Cal saw all that hard work turn into a lethal force on the front line.

"To my mind Alex is one of the most naturally gifted goal scorers in the history of soccer," Coach McGuire said. "She is a multi-dimensional striker. She can score with both feet using placement, power, or skill. She finds shooting space intuitively and is very strong in the air. What allowed her to be a world-class striker was her determination and work ethic to get there."

In late 2015, the NWSL expanded and added a

team, the Orlando Pride. Alex asked to be traded from Portland to Orlando because Servando was playing for Orlando City, of Major League Soccer (MLS). A deal was reached, and Alex set out trying to build up a fan base in Central Florida as she fought to grow the NWSL while getting to live like a somewhat normal couple. "For me to be able to live with my husband, I feel very fortunate," Alex said.

Then there was a little matter called the 2016 Olympics, which would take place in soccer-mad Brazil. With all the running around, the victory tour, the off-the-field obligations, and the NWSL duties, there was no time for rest. The US team got two weeks off between the end of the 2015 season and the start of the 2016 season.

"That's not nearly enough [time] to rest our legs, but there is not time between the World Cup and the Olympics to recover your mind and body," Alex said. "It's more about individually getting your mind right and re-sparking your passion."

The US easily qualified for the Olympics, outscoring its five opponents 23–0. Alex had four goals, including a hat trick in the semifinals. Alex had a strong season, scoring a couple goals in the She-Believes Cup in the spring, and then three more in a two-game Olympics tune-up series against Japan in July. Abby Wambach had retired, so Alex was now essentially alone on the front line, no longer benefitting from her "partner in crime." The positive was that she now had more room to operate and, potentially, more opportunities to shoot.

"It's different," Alex said. "I have to be more unpredictable in my runs, change things up because the defense is focused on me."

There were still plenty of talented teammates around her, including Carli Lloyd, Megan Rapinoe, and some young stars, such as Mallory Pugh and Julie Johnston. The US was still the top-ranked team in the world and the favorite to win gold. None of that changed when they rolled through group play, going 2–0–1, with Alex scoring once against New Zealand.

In the quarterfinals, the US matched up against Sweden, which was coached by Pia Sundhage, their old leader. Since taking over as coach, Pia had quickly built up the Swedish team. Lacking the firepower and deep talent pool she had when she coached the Americans, Pia employed a more conservative and defensive style with Sweden that could frustrate opponents. It would certainly frustrate the US.

The game was scoreless into the second half, with the Americans getting most of the chances but failing to convert. Sweden set up their players deep in their own territory, defending the goal and using extra bodies to jump into shooting lanes. They made little effort to run any sustained attack, hoping instead to capitalize on a US miscue. It worked. Not only was the US flustered, but in the sixty-first minute, Sweden scored on a counterattack. With Sweden's highly effective defensive style, no one knew if the US could come back.

Finally, in the seventy-seventh minute, Alex pounced on a loose ball about eight yards out in front of the net and drilled in a shot to tie it at 1–1. It was classic Alex—a big goal in a critical moment. The score stayed the same through extra sessions despite the US dominating the game. The Americans led in shots 27–6. The game came down to penalty kicks and Sweden won, 4–3. Out of nowhere, the powerhouse US team, the favorite to take home the gold, was knocked out of the Olympics without winning a medal.

The US was frustrated and humbled. This was not how the Olympics were supposed to go. Hope Solo lashed out at Sweden's style of play. "I thought we played a courageous game," she said. "I also think we played a bunch of cowards. The best team did not win today. I strongly, firmly believe that."

The comment set off a controversy and Hope was eventually suspended by US Soccer for a lack of sportsmanship. Pia, in her classic style, brushed off Hope's complaints. "I don't give a crap," Pia said. "I'm going to Rio [for the semifinals]. She's going home."

Alex was more diplomatic, but it wasn't easy stomaching the loss. The Olympics are the Olympics. She wanted to win. She also believed that up-tempo soccer was the key to growing the game. She gave full congratulations to Sweden, but she hoped this wasn't the future of the sport.

"It's not really that exciting for the fans when a team values defense so much," Alex said. "I want to make fans come back so I want to make it exciting. We want to have a lot of shots and some transition moments and counter moments. And when a team sits on the ball, that's not quite available. Can it be hurtful for the sport? I don't know. It's just a different style of soccer. I respect them all the same. It's just not always the most attractive to fans."

The worst part for Alex was that the early

departure from the Olympics meant there were almost three full years to sit and stew over the defeat until the 2019 FIFA Women's World Cup in France. Yes, there was the NWSL season and trying to win with her club in Orlando. Yes, she will play in friendlies and various cups, including SheBelieves. And yes, there will be more goals, and more appearances, and more people to inspire.

But deep down, from that first day in a rec game on a field back in Diamond Bar, all the way to getting cut by a travel team, finding Cypress Elite and reaching the US junior teams, through her ups and downs at Cal and the women's national team, she's been a competitor. She wants to win. She wanted to beat her older sisters in a footrace. She wanted to beat her parents in Monopoly. She wanted to beat out her rivals for a spot in the starting lineup. She wants to beat Japan or Sweden or Germany or anyone else who gets between her and a championship.

"I just can't imagine life without competition," she said.

That's what drives her. That's what has always driven her. That's what will continue to drive her throughout 2019 and beyond.

Instant Replay

The United States and Canada are tied in extra time of the Olympic semifinals.

US MIDFIELDER HEATHER O'REILLY RECEIVES THE BALL.

SHE CROSSES THE BALL TO ALEX.

THE PASS COMES ROCKETING TOWARD ALEX, WHO'S READY FOR THE HEADER!

The Nonstop Sports Action Continues!

Here's an excerpt of

EPIC ATHLETES
SIMONE BILES

Illustrations by Marcelo Baez

THE 2016 OLYMPICS WOMEN'S GYMNASTICS
ALL-AROUND FINAL

1

Golden

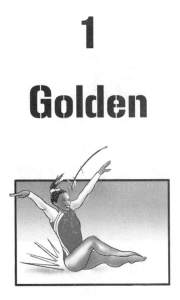

SIMONE BILES, IN HER custom-fit, red, white, and blue leotard, stood on one end of the mat, her left hand high in the air, her right resting on her hip.

Twelve thousand fans stared down at her inside Rio Olympic Arena in Brazil, everyone hushed and quiet as they waited for the music to start and Simone to begin a ninety-second floor routine that might tumble her right into history.

The then-nineteen-year-old from the suburbs of Houston, Texas, was in the lead at the women's all-around gymnastics competition at the 2016

Olympics. All that remained was her strongest event—floor. Do it well and she'd be crowned champion.

There were Olympic rings hanging on a banner overhead. There was a gold medal waiting to be hung around someone's neck. There was anticipation in the air as spectators wondered what type of show the greatest gymnast of all time would stage. She was a tiny figure in the middle of a huge arena, an American dynamo who stood just four foot eight.

"I tell people four foot nine sometimes," she once said with a laugh.

To say this was Simone Biles's lifelong dream, the one that powered her through the days at practice when she lacked motivation, wasn't even true. She had never actually dreamed this far. Olympic champion? Gold medalist? The greatest of all time? That was too much to conceive, even on those quiet nights growing up when she tried to fantasize her way to sleep.

No, as a young gymnast, leaping and cartwheeling through recreation classes and local Junior Olympic meets and even as she climbed the competitive national and international ranks, pushing herself more and more, she aspired only to reach the Olympics.

Just getting here was enough. Winning gold? It somehow never crossed her mind.

Simone was a planner. She liked to write down goals in a small notebook she kept in her bedroom back in Spring, Texas. It could be about achieving a certain grade in a certain class, something related to gymnastics, or another milestone. It was a way to keep her focused. It was a way to keep her going.

Yet once she qualified for her first Olympics a few weeks prior to the 2016 games in Rio de Janeiro, there was nothing else she had written down that remained to be accomplished. She had already been national champion four times and world champion three. She had already turned professional. She had already signed contracts that would make her millions in endorsement deals.

Her mother, Nellie, was concerned that Simone might not perform well if she didn't jot down the ultimate goal—Olympic champion in the all-around. That gold signifies the best in the world because it requires each gymnast to perform in all four events—vault, balance beam, uneven bars, and this one, floor exercise. So Nellie encouraged her daughter to put it on paper, make it official.

Simone was hesitant. It seemed unnecessary and

even made her nervous and anxious. She had come to embrace the philosophy of Martha Karolyi, the US national team coordinator and a legendary coach in the sport.

"Martha would say, 'You want to perform like you train. Did you perform like you trained? If you perform like you train, then the judging will work itself out,'" Simone said.

It's a simple lesson that can deliver incredible accomplishments. Do what you can do and don't stress about anything else.

"If I do my job, I do my job," Simone said. "There is nothing I can do to control the scores."

So Simone would only meet her mother halfway. She did write down a new goal, but it had nothing to do with medals or scores or sticking the landing on an Amanar.

"I will make you proud," Simone wrote to her mother.

That was it. That was all. Nellie could only smile when she read it. Simone could have fallen fifty times on her floor routine and she would still be proud of her daughter.

Ron and Nellie Biles were not Simone's birth parents. They were, originally, her grandparents.

Ron Biles had a daughter from a previous relationship named Shanon, who had given birth to four children, including Simone, the third child. Shanon and the kids lived in Ohio, but when Shanon struggled with alcohol and drug addiction, eventually child services said she was an unfit mother and took her children from her, putting them temporarily in foster care.

Ron and Nellie had married after his first relationship broke off, and they were living in Texas at the time. When Shanon was unable to care for her kids, the pair stepped in and adopted the two youngest, Simone and her little sister, Adria. The two older children went with another relative. It wasn't planned this way, but Grandma and Grandpa officially and legally became Simone's mom and dad. Ron and Nellie already had two older boys and now the family was unexpectedly bigger, and given Simone's natural interest in flips and twists, bouncier.

Neither Ron nor Nellie knew anything about gymnastics when Simone and Adria first began going to a local gym to burn off excess energy. They certainly never expected to be here, at the Olympics, staring down at their daughter who was on the verge of winning the all-around gold. It wasn't the athletic success that made them love her, though. It was everything else.

"We have so much satisfaction from all our kids," Ron Biles said. "We love family and everything involved with it. We share all the special moments together and this is a pretty special one."

Down on that mat, Simone was trying to remain calm. She had trained since she was six years old to get to this spot. She had always been a pint-size powerhouse, always small for her age. Yet in elementary school, she was often stronger than the boys and had no problem showing them.

She was pure muscle, with ripped arms and springy legs that launched her into the air. She had a core so strong she could twist in midair almost at will. She also possessed an unteachable ability to sense where she was while in flight.

The routine she was about to attempt was one of the most technically challenging runs of skills in the history of the sport. The Olympics were home to the best gymnasts on earth, yet no other gymnast present would even attempt such a difficult feat.

Simone wasn't just going to try it. She was going to try to do it perfectly.

It began with a full-twisting double layout, where

a gymnast flips in the air with her legs completely straightened out (rather than bending her knees). Next up, a double laid-out salto (a flip with the legs tucked to the chest) with a half twist, a move so hard that no one had ever landed it in a World Championship until Simone had done so in 2013. As a result, it was known as "the Biles."

The Biles led Simone into a split jump and later there was a tumbling pass with a double-double (two somersaults with two full twists) and then the finale with a tucked full-in (two somersaults and a twist with legs pressed together and to the chest). In between the four tumbling runs, there were other required moves, choreographed dancing with a salsa flair, and a beaming smile to engage the crowd.

The routine was so demanding that it earned a 6.800 degree of difficulty, which is one part of a gymnastics score. The other is how the judges think you executed it. No one else in the meet had a difficulty score higher than 6.600.

Simone hadn't lost an individual all-around competition since 2013, yet this one, the Olympic all-around, hadn't been easy. She had led after the first event, vault, but then fell behind Russia's Aliya Mustafina after the second rotation, bars, when

Aliya put up an impressive 15.666, a full 0.7 higher than Simone.

The crowd in Rio de Janeiro mumbled in surprise when Aliya took the overall lead, 30.866 to 30.832. Everyone had expected Simone to run away with the gold, just like always. Now they were wondering if a historic upset was in the making.

Simone's personal coach, Aimee Boorman, told her to just stick with her training. Teammate Aly Raisman, who was also competing in the all-around, high-fived her and tried to pump her up.

And Bela and Martha Karolyi, the legendary husband-and-wife coaching duo who essentially ran USA Gymnastics, reminded Simone that since bars were her weakest event and Aliya's strongest, there was no need to panic. There was plenty of time during the final two events—beam and floor—to retake the lead.

"That made this competition so spicy, so beautiful," said Bela Karolyi, who for over forty years had coached many of the greatest gymnasts of all time. "The beam is the leaning point [though]. The left or the right. The best-trained gymnast stays on the beam."

Well, beam was next. And before Simone's routine,

she heard Nellie Biles shout a saying that she'd been screaming to Simone her entire competitive career.

"You've got this, Simone!" Nellie said.

That was more than enough for Simone. As with the floor event to come, she benefited from having a far more difficult technical routine in the beam than her competitors, tougher than anyone else was even willing to attempt.

She then drilled it, proving herself, as Bela said, "the best-trained gymnast," and scoring a 15.433 to Aliya's 13.866.

Once again Simone was in the lead, this time by a commanding 1.533 points (while that may seem like a small margin, it's a *huge* lead in gymnastics).

By the time she stood on the mat to start her floor routine as the last performer of the night, she knew gold was there for the taking. Aliya's overall score had even been passed by Aly Raisman, thanks to Aly's tremendous execution on a very difficult floor routine.

Aly Raisman was competing in her second Olympics after winning a gold medal in 2012. She was famous and a hero to gymnasts around the world. Yet she knew that she wasn't going to beat Simone's score. Simone's lead was so large, and her routine so challenging, she could fall multiple times and still win.

Aly was fine with that. She, along with everyone else in attendance, knew there really was no competing with Simone Biles.

"[US teammate] Laurie Hernandez said to me, 'If you get silver, you're the best because Simone doesn't count,'" Aly said with a laugh. "Her start value is [so much] higher than me so I know I can't beat her."

Simone didn't like that kind of talk—she wanted to encourage her teammates. She loved them and was proud of how good they were. "I get more excited when they win," she said. When Aly finished her brilliant floor routine to assure her at least a silver medal, she cried in delight, with Simone hugging and celebrating with her.

Suddenly Simone was fighting back tears of joy for Aly. "I thought, 'Oh my God, she's going to make me cry before my floor,'" Simone later said with a laugh. "And that wasn't going to be good."

With what felt like the whole world watching Simone, it was not the time to think of Aly or anyone else. This was about doing what she had trained to do. This was the time to concentrate. This was the time to win.

As the music started, the anxiety melted away and a huge smile broke out on her face.

"That is all we needed to see," her older brother, Adam, who was also there cheering her on, said. "As long as she has a smile on her face, we know she is in a good place."

Soon she was sprinting down the mat for her first tumbling run and springing into her round-off. Her muscles were trained. Her mind was clear.

"Sometimes nothing goes through my mind," Simone said. "When I tumble, I just tumble."

She soared nearly ten feet into the air before landing cleanly, with just a small hop to take away the momentum. The crowd roared. Soon she was repeating it . . . the buildup of speed, the concentration, the flying toward glory before ending with a sound, sharp landing.

Just like that, Simone Biles knew she was going to win gold.

"Once the first two passes were out of the way, I knew I was good," she said.

Everyone knew. The crowd was now on its collective feet, waving flags and roaring in delight. This was the ultimate performance, a dream combination of skill and entertainment. Simone leaping. Simone flipping. Simone in total command.

"The joy," Bela Karolyi said of watching it. "The satisfaction."

"Pride," her dad said.

This is what Simone wanted—to perform for the beauty of performing. Not for judges. Not for medals. She had always loved gymnastics for the sake of gymnastics. She hadn't reached the national team until she was fifteen, late for the great ones. No one had ever doubted her ability, but coaches were frustrated that she sometimes wanted gymnastics to be more about fun than just work.

Simone liked to smile at practice. She liked to laugh. "Gymnastics is supposed to be fun," she'd say.

Eventually her performances got so good and her technical ability so precise that even Martha Karolyi gave up trying to rein her in. Martha was a taskmaster. She was forever pushing gymnasts to be better and better. She wasn't much for laughs and smiles during training.

Simone, though . . . well, Simone could pretty much do whatever she wanted. The performance, and the results, spoke for her.

"Simone Biles is the biggest talent," Martha said. "Combined with the very good discipline of work and great preparation for consistency, she is the best."

By the time her routine ended, Simone was beaming. She rushed off the mat and hugged Coach Aimee, hugged Martha, and eventually wound up in a prolonged hug with Aly. Four years prior, she'd watched Aly win team gold for the Americans at the 2012 London Olympics. Simone considered Aly a role model.

At the time, there was no guarantee that Simone would ever make the senior national team, or World Championships, or these Olympics. She was fifteen and still hadn't broken through. Now four years later, there they were, the two of them awaiting the final scores.

When the scores were presented, the pair hugged even tighter. Simone had scored a 15.933 on floor, the highest score by any competitor in any event that night. That meant she won all-around gold over Aly by a whopping 2.100 margin.

The 2.1 differential wasn't just the largest margin of victory in the history of the Olympic women's all-around. It was larger than the combined margins of victory of every Olympic all-around, 1980–2012. By comparison, Gabby Douglas won all-around gold in 2012 by just 0.259.

Simone had blown out the competition. She would climb atop the podium and receive her medal, and yet even with all that she'd accomplished, she said she didn't feel a whole lot different.

"I'm still the same old Simone," she said.

The road to gold hadn't been easy. It had been full of twists and turns, laden with doubts and down periods.

She had made it, though. She had fulfilled her goal of reaching the Olympics.

There was also that goal she'd written down in her notebook.

"I will make you proud," she had promised her mother.

Up in the stands, with her parents and siblings crying tears of happiness, there was no doubt she had done that, too.

Hungry for More EPIC ATHLETES?
Look Out for These Superstar
Biographies, in Stores Now!